Chico's
ORGANIC GARDENING
AND NATURAL LIVING

Chico's
ORGANIC GARDENING AND NATURAL LIVING

by Frank ("Chico") Bucaro

and David Wallechinsky

J. B. LIPPINCOTT COMPANY
Philadelphia and New York

U.S. Library of Congress Cataloging in Publication Data

Bucaro, Frank, birth date
  Chico's organic gardening and natural living.
  1. Organiculture.   2. Cookery, Italian.
I. Wallechinsky, David, birth date   II. Title.
III. Title: Organic gardening and natural living.
S605.5.B8   635'.048   70-37611
ISBN-0-397-00758-2
ISBN-0-397-00885-6 (pbk.)

FOR BEA

CONTENTS

8   *Contents*

INTRODUCTION

My name is Frank Bucaro, but everybody know me by Chico. I was born on a farm in Sicily in 1900. My childhood was spent living on farms with my family in Italy, Tunisia and Algeria. Most of what I know about growing food, I learned from my family, and the rest from my own experience.

I made my living many ways after I grew up: selling produce from a pushcart, being a magician, working in a factory, being a soldier, selling gardenias, sitting on a volcano listening for signs of an eruption to warn the people, and running a nursery.

In 1959 my wife and I bought five and a half acres on the corner of Pacific Coast Highway and Morning View Drive near Zuma Beach in Los Angeles. Here we grow organic fruits, nuts, beans and vegetables and sell them to people who come by.

The last couple years lots of young people have started to come to my farm to learn how to run a farm and how to raise food organically.

Now I think it is time to share some of my knowledge with as many people as want to learn. I don't know how to read or write, so I have taught what I know to David and he has made it into a book. I hope that older people will be helped by this book, not just young people.

ANOTHER INTRODUCTION

My name is David Wallechinsky, and I became interested in organic foods when I realized that the corporate farms which grow most of America's produce do not care at all about my health.

While driving near the Salton Sea in Southern California, I passed the orchard of a famous corporate fruit grower which was guarded by a sign that read STAY ALIVE, STAY OUT.

I soon felt an urge to learn how to raise food myself and not be dependent on big businesses. But I was brought up in urban and suburban areas and knew nothing of farming. I wished that there was a book to help me on my way. Then I met Chico, and he wanted to write a book.

Of course the only way to learn how to grow foods is to do it, so I hope that this book will help move people out of the house and into the garden. Treat the plants lovingly and don't feel confined by rules and measurements. Keep experimenting.

Chico's
**ORGANIC GARDENING
AND NATURAL LIVING**

1

WHY ORGANIC GARDENING?

WHY GROW A GARDEN?

David answers:

1. Home-grown food costs less and tastes better.

2. Freshly picked foods are far more nutritious than store-bought foods that have to be picked before they are ripe so they will look nice in the market.

3. It is a spiritually exhilarating experience to tend a garden, watching the changes day by day.

4. Eating a vegetable that you have known intimately for three or four months is more fulfilling than eating a vegetable that has an unknown background.

5. Presently in the United States, most food is manufactured (not grown) by huge corporate farms that treat the plants not as living things but as something to make money from. There is little concern about providing food to make a healthy nation. For most people involved in the growing

process, this is understandable. Times are hard and workers are thankful to have any job at all. But for the corporate leaders who reap the profits of agribusiness (as it is known in big business circles), this lack of concern for the quality of their product is despicable. Until the time comes when corporate lands are expropriated and redistributed to people who work the land themselves, growing a garden is one way to lessen one's dependence on uncaring corporations.

WHY ORGANIC?

David answers:

When a plant is grown organically, it means that the fertilizers used are natural instead of chemical and that pest control is done without the use of harmful insecticides.

1. Organic food-growing uses waste products (leaves, weeds, garbage, sludge, grass clippings, hair, human and animal waste) that chemical food-growing relegates to garbage dumps and oceans.

2. Organic food tastes better and is richer in nutrients.

3. Organic gardening helps the gardener learn about the cycles of life and increases awareness of man's place in nature.

4. Avoiding dangerous chemicals makes the house or farm safer. Four out of five pesticide accident victims are less than five years old, and in Florida pesticides are the leading cause of death for the under-five-year age group.

Organic methods are natural and have been used for millennia. On the other hand, the most commonly used pesticides are of recent invention and the long-term effects are unknown. The chemical industry and agribusiness are using us as guinea pigs without consulting us.

The greatest victims of chemical sprays are farm workers who are exposed to excess amounts of poison through errors, experimentation, normal procedures and general insensitivity of growers whose obsession with profits leads them to treat workers and, to a lesser extent, the rest of us who eat the food they manufacture and breathe the air they pollute, not as human beings, but as objects to be manipulated.

Chico answers:

When I lived in Italy, we ate mostly spaghetti with different wild vegetables and herbs. Also we ate sometimes fruit, cheese and, once a year, meat. None of the food was grown with chemicals. Even if anyone in our town had wanted to use chemicals, no one had enough money to buy them. And all the time I was in Italy, until I was twenty-three, I never was sick except once when I was a baby.

When I came to America, I settled with my brother and his family and we ate meat, sweets and a lot of heavy things. In three weeks my face turned yellow and I didn't feel so good.

The longer I lived in America, the more illnesses I got until ten years ago, when I was suffering colitis, arthritis, hay fever, hemorrhoids, fistula and asthma. I don't know what there is that I didn't have.

I used to have a flower shop, and the day before St. Patrick's Day we used to put white carnations in water with green coloring. The next morning the carnations were green because they had been drinking the green water.

That made me think that plants that are sprayed with poison must drink the poisons from the water, the soil and the air. So I started to be organic like I used to be in Italy. But the city puts chlorine in the water, and chlorine is a poison. My wife uses it to bleach clothes. So I made my own well so my plants could have pure water.

I cured myself with the food and herbs that I grew on my land. Now all my illnesses are gone, except for a little arthritis, and I'll never use chemicals again.

2

SOIL

My name is Frank Bucaro, but everybody know me by Chico.

First we will talk about soil, but I will only talk about the kinds of soil I am familiar with.

To test the soil, no matter where you are, get a handful of damp soil and squeeze it as hard as you can. Then put your thumb on top of the soil and push it down and try to break it. If the soil falls apart and crumbles, that's more or less good soil. If the soil stays in a lump when you squeeze it and, when you try to break it, it sticks on your hand and thumb, that's also good soil, but you have to add food to it.

If your soil is sticky, it is probably adobe (clay). I would put about 2 or 3 inches of hay or fertilizer on top and turn it over about a foot deep. After that, if you are in a dry climate, water about every second day for two weeks. Give it a good soaking. If you are in a moist climate, water the soil when it starts to get pretty dry. After two weeks you turn the soil again, level it and plant. That's if it is summertime. If it is winter, the rain will take care of it.

If your soil is granite, it is good soil but it has no good food. You have to add your own food. When you water granite, the water goes right down. So you have to add a lot of fertilizer: horse manure, cow manure, any kind of fertilizer that is low in nitrogen and makes mulch. You see, you only want soil that is loose and moist. Granite soil is loose, because, like adobe, if you walk on it, it will pack. I walk as little as possible on granite or adobe.

Treat granite like adobe. Add manure, turn it over (never less than a foot), water every two days, and after two weeks turn it over again and plant.

If you have sandy soil, like around Ohio and Indiana, it is the best soil there is because it won't pack tight and the roots can travel. If you are inexperienced and you are looking for soil, that's what I would look for.

With sandy soil, you have to add nitrogen and potash and everything else yourself. I would put about 2 or 3 inches of hay and 1 or 1½ inches of fertilizer on top and turn it over. Then do the same process: water it, turn it over again and plant. That way you'll have good soil for at least five years.

We've been talking about people who have a small planting area. If you have a big farm—five, ten, twenty, a hundred acres, whatever you have—what I would do is, the first year, right after it rains, throw any kind of fertilizer and let the weeds grow. When they get 3 to 4 feet, before they get dry, turn them under with a plow, Rototiller, disk or whatever you have.

If you are on your property a year before you want to plant, plow it all and don't do nothing with it. When the rain comes, the soil starts to throw a lot of different weeds. Let them grow as high as possible. I let them grow 4, 5, even 6 feet. They been so high sometimes that my wife been looking for me and I'm with the tractor plowing and she couldn't see me.

Turn the soil in, wait a month and turn it in again, because new weeds start growing. I would turn it in two or three times. From then on you will have the best soil you been looking for, and you can plant whatever you want to. And you repeat this every three years or else you fertilize heavy every year.

Watch out for red soils because they usually have acid. Sometimes they won't, but nine out of ten they will. Very few things like to grow in acid: some flowers, like fuchsias, gardenias and rhododendrons, but not food crops. If they do grow, they grow very skinny and never amount to anything. I never did find a red soil that was good for farming. In Arizona and Texas you see acres and acres of red and dusty soil and they never grow nothing.

Suppose you are in a place that is all pure sand. You can raise most anything and it will mature early because the sand is hot and the plants like that. You can even raise summer crops in winter. But you have to put a strong fertilizer like chicken or rabbit manure in the sand, because the sand doesn't have good food of any kind. I would add wood ashes too. Then you turn it over and you have good soil to plant things. When I had sand properties we grew early tomatoes before anyone else. But it takes a lot of work and a lot of water.

If you are back East, like New York or the Midwest, there is usually a lot of black and pink clay that you can make bricks out of. If you know how to handle adobe, it is very good for growing food too. If you work it when it is muddy, it is too sticky, and if you work it when it is dry, it is too hard and it won't break. You have to catch it between dry and wet. If there is rain for two or three days, a week and a half later you go out and plow. Wait until it is half dry, but before it gets cracks. If the soil gets too hard, you can't break it and there will be big lumps.

If you have a farm with pink clay I would mix a hundred-pound sack of gypsum into every twenty-five hundred square feet. If you have hay or straw, put that in too. Then plow it under. With a small farm or garden that you work by hand, the soil has to be looser, so I would put a hundred-pound sack of gypsum every 625 square feet.

The gypsum makes it less sticky when it is wet. It makes it looser. The hay or straw loosens the soil. The plants like that because they don't have to press hard when the roots start traveling.

If you do like I been talking, you'll have good service.

Now, every year you don't put the same plants on the same spot. If you put beans one year, you put corn or wheat there next year. Try to plant each crop at least two hundred or three hundred feet away from where you planted it last year. The reason for this is that different plants eat different kinds of food from the soil, and the soil needs time to rest and build up more food.

If there is a swamp where you are and the water stands in the swamp all winter, you can plant there after all the water is gone and it is good and dry. Don't ever plant before the rain because the seeds get rotten and moldy and die. They never grow. After the rainy season is over, then you can plant. Usually a swamp has good soil because all the water that runs over the swamp brings minerals and food from all around. But you have to know what you're doing.

If you haven't already got your property, I would stay away from adobe and swamp and places with big rocks. Choose a level spot. Granite soil is good, but sandy soil is best, and that's what I would look for.

3

PREPARING SOIL
AND BEGINNING SEED

What we are going to talk about now is how you mix your soil to put the seed in commercially or for yourself.

You take a box, or what we call a flat. A flat is a box 18 by 18 inches and 2 inches deep. Flats are made of redwood, because redwood has a little acid in it and the plants like a little acid. If you haven't got that particular box, you go to any nursery and they will have it and they will sell it to you. Buy extra flats because you will need a lot of them when you start transplanting.

How do you mix soil? In a wheelbarrow make a mixture of 2 parts horse or cow or rabbit or human manure, 1 part peat moss, 1 part leaf mold, 1 part sand, 1 part loam soil, 1 part fine gravel, ¼ cup bone meal, ¼ cup blood meal and ¼ cup wood ashes. Then you have a good mixture to raise small seeds in the flats.

This soil has to be screened very fine because if there is a little lump in the soil, the seed will just pop off from the germ and it will grow crooked and you will lose the plant.

With this particular soil mixture and good seed, 95 percent will germinate. You can do it an easier way if you don't care how many plants come up out of the soil. You can use any kind of soil or you can plant right in the rows, but then you get from 10 to 15 percent seed coming up unless it rains right away. Then you get 75 percent.

In each flat you can raise eight varieties of seed, but you should separate them with little sticks and label them.

But if you are raising commercially, I recommend you put only one variety of seed in each flat, because when you raise commercially, you have to have a field of mostly one kind. And if you make one-half flat celery and one-half flat lettuce, the seeds will mix together. But for yourself you can do like I just said.

Then you sprinkle the seed very lightly and be sure that you don't put the seeds in clumps. Each seed should be separate. You can put three hundred seeds or more in each flat. Then you get a little bit of soil and sprinkle it on top of the seeds as lightly as possible. No more than ¼ inch.

Every morning you have to sprinkle the flat with water lightly without fail. You have to make a real habit in the morning, and sometimes in the evening. Make sure you sprinkle very light because a heavy stream will knock down the soil and disturb the seed coming up. If it is very light, they will grow even and perfect. Sometimes people give too much water and it is necessary to drain the flats, but if you make sure to include fine gravel in your soil mixture, you won't have that problem.

Then you let them grow in the flat until they get 3½ to 4 or 5 inches. I don't let them grow any higher. And you transfer them to another flat with the same mixture of soil. In that flat you put a hundred plants and you let them grow there for another month.

Now, when you transplant them into this second flat you put
them in the shade under a tree, in a protected place. No
wind, no sun for the first four days. If it is cold at night,
cover them up or bring them inside. After the four days, you
put them in direct sun. Now remember that you have to
water every morning and every evening, the same like you do
when they are in the first flat, because if you don't you lose
half or more.

After you have them in the sun for at least two weeks, then
you can plant them in the field. Now the reason to move
them to another flat is so that the plant gets used to being
transferred. Also, when you transfer the plant, you give a little
soil with the plant. You can't do this with the first flat because
the seeds grow too close together. When there is no chance to
give any soil with the plant you transfer, that plant will suffer.
But when you have a little soil with the plant, it won't suffer.

Another way you can do that is, if it is wintertime (or spring
in areas where there are cold winters), you wet the flat and
the plants until the soil is soupy. Tap all four sides of the flat
and all four corners. See that the soil is all loose from the flat
and from the roots of the plant. Then you get a bucket and
mix some mud in it. Take the plants from the flat and mix
them with the mud. Shake the roots in the mud and let the
mud get in every part of the roots. Then you can plant in the
field. That way you gain three weeks. That's if you know how.
I would not recommend that you do this in the summer because the hot sun will burn the plants. I do recommend the
way I said before: to put them in another flat, so you won't
have any trouble. But still you water every morning for at least
a week or a week and a half. Now remember that. Don't you
ever forget about that. When you transplant plants they have
to be watered every morning and sometimes two or three
times a day, depending how the weather is. That way you
get 85, 95, 100 percent plants. Because if you do buy seed

that is pretty expensive, every seed you lose is food coming out of your mouth.

What we been talking about is for small seed like cauliflower, broccoli, celery, spinach, spice or any kind of small seed. But the big seeds like beans, corn, squash or melon, you don't have to plant them in the flat. The big seeds you can plant right in the field.

To prepare the field, you throw compost, hay, fertilizer—whatever you have—on the field you are going to plant. If it is a big field you can put hay, which is cheaper. Use anything you can get hold of to keep the ground moist. If you have enough water, you water the field for a week just like if you had plants. Then you turn the ground inside and out, the top on the bottom and bottom on the top. And that ground should be turned over at least 8 inches, and more would be better.

Now if it is a small piece of ground you have, you keep on watering for two weeks every morning and every evening just like if you had plants. Now the reason for that is, if there is any wild seed in there, it will come up. Then you let it sit three to five days and you turn it over again. And you make your rows.

Try to make your rows as level as possible. No slope. If you haven't got level ground, adjust your ground. Curve your rows so each row will be level. Then you plant your plants in the rows you been making. The reason to not have slope is because, when you water, the water stays with the plants instead of washing right off.

If you are in a place with dry weather and no humidity, like around here in Malibu, you've got to put the plants in between the rows, not on the top, so when you water, the plants get the water.

If you are in a place where there is a lot of moisture in the air, where the ground is always damp, you can put them on

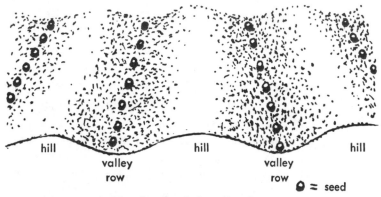

Planting Seeds in a Dry Area

top of the hills. Not between the rows, on top of the rows. And when you water them, you water between the rows and the plants will drink.

But in a dry area, always put them in the center of the row. I would stagger them in the row, so you'll have more room, if you have a small planting area. If you've got a big field, it won't be necessary. You can put them in the center or on the

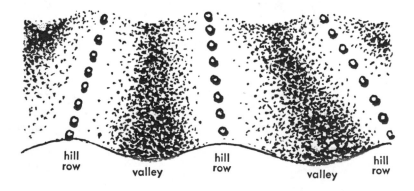

Planting Seeds in a Moist Area

top, if you've got the moisture. You don't have to stagger them. If you haven't got much room to plant, you stagger the plants and by staggering you gain 8 inches on each plant.

Depending on what kind of plant it is, you have to space them in the rows. Cauliflower should be 12 to 14 inches in either direction. Celery should be 6 to 8 inches. But not tomatoes. Tomatoes should be 36 to 60 inches apart. Broccoli should be 10 to 12 inches.

Now when you come to melon, melon should be from 3 feet to 40 inches apart. The same with squash, cucumbers and pumpkins. And when you plant anything large, don't put one seed in each hole; you put three or four or five because not all of them seeds are going to germinate. Maybe you'll get one out of five, maybe you'll get five. Then when they start growing, you leave two and pull out the rest. Remember that with all the plants of the vine, you got to give them space. No question about it. If you don't give them any space, you are in trouble for a lot of reasons. One reason is that the plants grow close together, cover each other up and no sun gets in there and the flowers won't germinate. Another reason is that, whatever the plant is, it will never come back because it is too crowded together. If you separate like I said to, you have a good ripe crop.

4

UNDERSTANDING PLANTS
AND TRANSFERRING

Now you have to understand the plants. That's what we're going to talk about, because you have to love a plant for it to live for you. But you can't love with just your mind. You have to love with your heart, with your mind and with your brains.

You can't love a plant because it's going to give you food. You got to love the plant because it is a plant. It is life. If you do love the plant because it is life, not because it gives you something in return, the plant will talk to you. She'll tell you when she needs water, when she needs food, and she'll tell you when she is sick.

Now, how can you tell if she needs water? As you pass by and you see the plant, if the plant is drooping, mushy like, that plant needs water. Now if the plant is real mushy all the way to the tip, don't give it too much water because you'll make it sick. You got to give it water a little bit at a time until the tips of the plant stands up. Remember that it takes at least three hours for the plant to drink all the water. From then on, keep it damp, but don't drown it. If the soil is wet, don't water; if it is dry, give a little water.

If the plant is sick because something is wrong in the roots, the plant looks droopy; the leaves start to look yellow and pale and then they fall down. If the plant needs food, the plant is a different kind of yellow than when she is sick. The yellow is a little deeper, but dry yellow, not life yellow. If you just tell the plant you're going to take care of her, she will live a little longer. She'll wait for you to put the food or the water

But if there is something wrong in the roots, there is nothing you can do about it except you cut most of the branches on top, very close. If it is a tree 8 to 10 feet high and about 8 feet spread, you cut about 4 feet on each branch and leave a little fork on each branch all the way around the tree and on the top.

If it is an old fruit tree, about 15, 18, 20 feet high and the same spread, you can tell if it is going to die two years from now. Two years before they die, they are going to throw a lot of fruit, lots of fruit, and they're going to hold it all on the tree. Usually some of the fruit drops when the tree is healthy. (Sometimes a tree is very healthy and strong and holds all the fruit and you have to take some of the fruit off.) But if your tree is sick and knows he's going to die, he will hold a lot of fruit. And the fruit is going to be small and the tree starts to get pale. Not dark green; they start looking yellow-green the first year. But they do give you a lot of fruit. Small, not big.

The second year they give you a little less fruit and the tree looks more sick than the first year. Now, don't wait until the second year if the tree does that. Because then it will be too far gone. Everybody thinks that because the tree makes a lot of fruit that it's healthy, but it's on its way out.

Now, if the tree has yellow leaves and pale leaves, that means the tree is on its way out. Something is wrong with

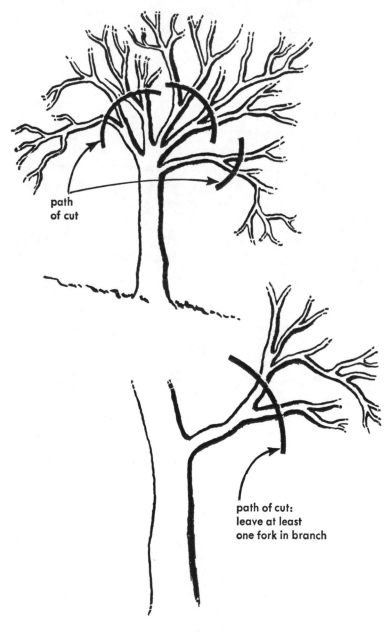

path
of cut

path of cut:
leave at least
one fork in branch

Pruning Sick Trees

the root system. We're talking about a tree that's about 20 feet high and 20 feet spread. If you want to help that tree, you got to cut the branches at least 5 feet or more all the way around and on the top. But always cut near the fork. Leave about 3 inches from the fork. All the way around.

Then you cut down on the water. Because the tree is sick doesn't mean it needs water. Watch it carefully. Dig a hole in the ground and see if it is damp. If it is, the tree doesn't need water; it is sick. Sometimes you'll have the same reaction if the tree needs nitrogen, potash, iron sulfate or food. But not like when the tree is sick.

You got to try and understand the tree and the leaves. If you look at the leaves and you do love them, you'll understand them. But if you don't love them, don't bother. I've seen people who love their plant because they want that plant, not because they actually love the plant but because somebody else has one. If he need to dig it out, he won't because he don't feel like it. Or if it needs water and the water is far away to get with the bucket, he won't go down there. He says, "Well, I haven't got time right now." He loves with the brains, but not with the heart.

Now if it is me, for instance, if my wife calls me for dinner, when she call me, I got to be there. If I'm not there, she starts to throw things around. But if I see a plant that needs water, I go and get the hose or the bucket. I take care of the plant first. I give it a drink before I have my supper. That's the way you love the plants. Not by if you're hungry and you got four or five plants that need water, so you tell yourself, "Oh, I'll go back there later and put some water." You'll forget about it. You go eat and something else turns up.

Some plants, even when they are real dry, will live, depending on how much humidity is in the air. But with other plants, an hour makes a lot of difference. You never can pick up those plants any more. That's especially true for young shoot plants. If it's a little vegetable plant, if you don't water her when she needs it, she will die.

When the plant is sick, don't ever feed it. You can give them love, but don't feed them or give them too much water. It's just like human beings. If you're going to die, you're going to die. But sometimes, by giving them enough love, plants will live. Also human beings. But if you don't care for that plant, if you don't pay attention to it, that plant hasn't got nothing to live for. It will die. That's the truth.

Also, you have the same reaction when you transfer a plant from one place to another. Be sure that you transfer the plant at the right time. Make sure a plant is dormant, that it has dropped all its leaves; don't try to dig it out until all the leaves are gone. Some people say, "I haven't got time. I have to move. I'm going to take the plant with me." Don't bother. It will die. If you have to move, you make an agreement with the people who are going to move in there that you want the plant. You wait for wintertime, or early spring; that's the time to pull plants that are dormant.

When you start to dig it out, give it all the roots you can. I never give them less than 3 feet of roots. Of course, that's if it is a plant that is about 8 to 10 feet high. If it is a small plant, it won't matter. You give them about 5, 6, 7 inches of root. It depends how big the plant is. Try not to bruise the roots. Dig it out all the way around very carefully. When you got it all dug out, cut the roots sharp. All the way around. Then you cut the branches. If a plant is 3 feet high, I would cut each tip 2 inches all the way around. If it is 10 feet high, cut each tip 1 foot. That way, it won't suffer. You do that because the plant goes to sleep in the wintertime. Dormant. That's the way you got to transfer—when they're sleeping. So when the plant wakes up, no matter where you put her, she keeps on growing just like she was before you moved her. She won't know that she been moved and she'll grow good.

But if you do move them when the leaves have started, because nobody told you or because you forgot about it or because you didn't have time, don't bother to move them because she knows you cut her off. She's in pain and she starts to bleed and she'll die. Exactly like a human being. If you have an operation without any ether or anesthetic, you can't stand the pain—and believe me, I know, because they cut on me without giving me any ether, without putting me to sleep. And I was hollering like a mad dog. A plant is the same thing.

Now, if there is a shrub or tree that you want to move that is a perennial, you wait for the tree to go dormant in a different way. The way you know when to move them is when the tree makes seed and the seed is pretty well ripe and drops down. Or the seed is well matured on the tree. Don't try to transfer them when they have blossoms and young shoots. We're talking about the perennials, that have leaves all year around. Let's say an orange or other citrus tree. You move the orange tree when all the fruit is gone. Wait about a month after the fruit is gone, but before new shoots and blossoms start. If it is a tree that has leaves all year around, like an olive tree, when all the olives are gone, around October or November, then in December you can try to pull it out. But leave all the roots you can.

At the same time that you pull it out, prune that tree. Don't leave any branches uncut. Take all the excess branches off. Thin down in the center and thin down on top. Don't leave too much branches, because then it will have too much to support and the tree can't take care of itself. They haven't got no energy to take care when you transfer because they haven't got enough roots. And because they will be sick for a while.

Don't feed a tree when you transfer. That's real important. You water them a little bit at a time. Don't ever give too much water. If you do, the tree will drown. But still you have to water it a little bit at a time. Or if you give it food, that tree will die. Because when you move the tree from one place to another, it's just the same as when a doctor gives an operation.

When a doctor operates on you, they put you in bed, they give you soup. They start dinner with a little soup. They won't feed you steak right after the operation. The same thing with the tree. You don't feed them heavy; you don't give much food at all. But you do give them a little bone meal. Depending on how big the tree is when you transfer, you give one or two handsful. You put some in the ground before you put the tree on top of the hole. Then you get some bone meal and put it around the tree. Then you cover it up with the soil. I always like to put soil that is a mixture of half sand and half soil. And pack it in when you plant it. You water them once and forget them for a while. Depending on how the weather is.

If it is dry weather, after a week put in a little water. Not too much. Enough to keep them alive. If it is damp, low clouds, fog, don't give them any water. Of course, if it rains, the rain will take care of it. I usually give rainwater to a tree that I transfer. I trap rainwater and I give that, because the rainwater hasn't got anything. It hasn't got no iron. It's not alkaline and it's not acid. Rainwater is neutral. That's what I give to the sick tree and the tree that has moved.

I always have two or three empty barrels under the eaves of my house and garage, and when it rains I trap the water. I keep it and use it when I need it for something unusual. Again, I don't like to have any barrel that is iron because it will rust and drop some iron in the water. And when the plant is sick, it don't like anything until it gets over the sickness. I put a wood barrel or big plastic barrel and I keep that water all year around. I never use that water except in emergency. If you do that, you can depend that the plant, no matter what it is, will live for you.

You do the same thing when you buy plants in the nursery. When you buy plants in the nursery, any kind of plant, like plum trees, you cut 3 or 4 inches from the top and you cut a couple inches off the roots all the way around. The simple reason you cut the roots is the roots are sealed. Any kind of plants, when you cut them, seal themselves after three or four hours. When you plant them you have to open the surface. You cut another 2 or 3 inches, so the surface opens and she starts to drink the water from the ground and come back to life. But if you don't cut that, sometime they live, sometime they don't. But most of the time, they don't. I've had trees that stay alive for two years, but they won't do anything. They will die. But when you cut the roots, they'll live. That's if you buy bare roots.

If you do buy trees or bushes or shrubs, I recommend buying them in a can because that way you gain one year. You can tell the nurseryman to cut the can. Be sure to let him cut it. Don't cut them yourself. Of course, again, if you're going to take this plant out of the state or out of the county, and you won't plant the same day that you buy it, don't cut the can, because when you cut the can, the roots get air, especially the little roots that been cut off, and they suffer.

Whenever you cut the can, the plant or tree has to be planted. The way you plant them is you make a hole about two times as big as the can. About two or three times wider, if it is small, and two or three times deeper. Then you fill the hole with loose or good soil way up to the height of the can. Fill it up without packing. For example, if you have a 4-foot hole, put in 2 feet of loose soil, take the plant out of the can and put it in the hole. Then add more soil, leaving a trench around the top. If you have the can already cut, open it up very carefully. To cut your own can, make two cuts, opposite each other, from top to bottom. Open up one side first, lie it down and then open the other side. When it is well open, you put your hands in the can. Lift up the plant and put it in the soft soil you put in the hole.

Then you put a handful bone meal. I'm talking about a one-gallon-can plant. If it is a five-gallon can, you put two handsful. If it is a ten-gallon can, you put four handsful bone meal all the way around. Then you put your soil around the ball (what has been inside the can), and you fill it up and pack it. Leave a little trench all the way around. When you do that you give water. Fill up the trench with water. If it is a one-gallon can I leave a trench about 2 feet away from the trunk. If it is five-gallon can, I leave 3 feet away from the trunk. And about 4 to 6 inches high. So they can hold that much water on the tree. If you do that and fill it up once, you don't have to worry about it. Otherwise, if it is hot weather, you have to water it every second day. This way you can stay three or four weeks without bothering it. But if you don't leave the trench, you got to water often. That's the way I do it if I really love the tree.

Then you ask me when I am going to feed the tree. You feed the tree or bush when it starts to throw new leaves or branches. Not until it shoots new branches. And you wait until the branch grows 4 or 5 inches. Then you can start to feed them. I would mix, especially if it is a fruit tree, one part bone meal, one part blood meal and one part potash. That's for fruit trees. If it is not a fruit tree, don't bother with the potash.

After you feed them, you water them good. You have to water them often after you feed them. For instance, if you been watering them once every two or three weeks, then you water them every week. For at least three waterings. After the plant has had food and been watered three times, you can water regular again. You water first, before you put the food in there and she grabs the food all at once and she gets sick. You have to remember that.

5

TOMATOES FROM ROWS
TO HARVEST

Now we're going to talk about after you transfer the plants to rows from the flats. Let's say you plant tomatoes. First, let me say that my favorite kind of tomatoes are beefsteak, which is big, juicy and solid, and Pearson Improved, which gives a perfect round shape and won't crack.

After you transfer the tomatoes to the row, you let them go in the row for two or three weeks and water them every morning. Watch them to make sure they are doing all right. Now remember this: when you transfer, never let the leaves touch the ground because they won't be able to breathe right and they will rot.

For the first two or three days, sprinkle very light and often. Watch every morning before you start watering. When they start to get flowers, don't water them too much like you used to. You don't have to sprinkle any more. Instead, water in the row, because if you get the flowers wet, the moisture will get in the flowers and they will drop off.

And put in stakes when the tomato plants get the size of 1 foot. Put in stakes about 4 or 5 feet tall and tie the vines up on the stake. The plant always should be off the ground because if it is on the ground, the leaves get rot, bugs hide under there, and the tomatoes themselves they don't like it.

I would say after the tomato vines get flowers, you water once a week if it don't rain. After they start to make tomatoes, once every three weeks put a gallon of seawater in a bucket for each hundred-foot row and let it run out into the row by putting a running hose of sweet water in the bucket. The day before you do this, water the rows with regular water so that the plants won't be thirsty and drink all the salt at once. Do this any time you add fertilizer too. Adding the seawater makes the tomatoes sweet and good-flavored. If you can't get real seawater, buy some sea salt at a natural foods store and mix it in a bucket with plain water.

When the tomato vines start to make little tomatoes, you dust them with one part each dusting sulfur, lime, bone meal and wood ashes. You go to the nursery and buy dusting sulfur. Sulfur is not poison. I don't know if your mother ever gave you sulfur molasses when you had a cold; you didn't die. It didn't harm you, it helped you. Also, it helps the plants. In fact, in my opinion, you can put sulfur on any kind of plant. But not when it is tender, because sulfur will burn tender plants a little bit. It will burn the tip. The advantage you get from the sulfur is you don't get fungus, you don't get mealy bugs, and no ants will go near where there is a lot of sulfur. It won't kill them, but it discourages them. That sulfur will keep away the ants, the little bugs and the big green bugs that got horns. I would dust once every twenty-five days, but remember this: don't ever water on the top any more. Don't ever wet the leaves after the tomatoes have started growing. If it rains, you have to dust again.

If you see a tomato plant that don't grow good, the leaves

are all wrinkled up and they stop growing—pull it out. The tomato plant, he's got fungus that you can't cure. And those particular tomatoes, they will give disease to the others. I would pull them and burn them or take them as far away from the other tomatoes as possible. Don't put them in the compost, if you do have compost, because the disease will carry on.

When the tomatoes get hard and high, you tie them up on the stick.

When the tomato plants get lots of leaves, you take off all the big leaves that cover the little tomatoes. You leave about four or five leaves at the top. You take off the old leaves so all the strength goes to the flowers and tomatoes and so the sun can come in and the tomatoes get ripe faster. You'll get big tomatoes and lots of tomatoes.

I want to point this out. Tomatoes like strong nitrogen food, like for instance you can put strong hot chicken manure or rabbit manure every fifteen days. If you want, you can put blood meal at least once every twenty days.

Now, how do you put the chicken manure on the tomatoes? You get a bucket, you put chicken manure in the bucket. Then you put a hose inside the bucket where the chicken manure is and let it overflow and run in the row so that the chicken manure goes to the tomatoes as liquid manure. Let it run evenly on the rows. Remember to water the rows the day before you feed them.

Or you can put liquid fish fertilizer the same way: you put it in the bucket and let it run. But any plants you have to fertilize, do it when the plant is young, not when the plant is old. Because when it is too old, the plant never takes the fertilizer any more. You have to help the plant when it is a baby. When it is a baby, you water with the fertilizer. If it is losing color, do it after two weeks. If the plant is still dark green after two weeks, wait until day 20. You'll have a strong, hardy plant, and when it start to make fruit, it makes perfect fruit, good tasting and big. Fertilize until the tomatoes start to get ripe. After you see a few ripe tomatoes, don't feed any more, because sometimes you taste the fertilizer that you been putting on the tomatoes or any other plants.

Of course, don't ever put any chemical fertilizer. I would recommend liquid fish, chicken (you make your own liquid), rabbit (you make your own liquid). But not horse manure. Horse or cow manure, you can put in the ground. Put it in before you plant. That's for tomatoes and other vegetables.

When you start to pick tomatoes, it doesn't matter if the tomatoes are not completely red because all the flavor has been given to the tomato by the time it gets pink. And if you let them get red, the birds and the bugs, when they see an attractive color like red, they will attack.

So you put the tomatoes in a box and put them in a shady place. You cover them with paper or with a gunnysack until they are ripe enough to suit you.

If you are East where it's real cold, where it freezes, you pick all the tomatoes before the frost. You do this so the tomatoes won't freeze on the vine, because when tomatoes freeze, they're no good any more. Use the ripe tomatoes and put the green ones in a box. You put them in the cellar and you put a wet sack over the box. I would wet the sack once every two or three days. Keep the sack wet so the tomatoes don't wrinkle or get soft and mushy and so they have just as much dampness as if they were on the mother. When you pick them and you put them in a protected place, they will ripen, all of them. Even if you put a wet sack only once a week, the tomatoes still will ripen. That's if it is in a place where there is frost.

Now, around here, you don't have to do that. Around here in California, we have tomatoes most all winter if you cover them up with plastic or anything that will protect them at night if it might frost. Tomatoes, potatoes, eggplant and pepper should be picked before frost. That's very simple. But with the other plants, it don't matter.

When you pick tomatoes green, see that you have a piece of stem with the tomatoes. I would say about two inches. Then you will have full flavor. If you take the stem off the tomatoes, they will ripen but they won't have any flavor. Those are the tomatoes you buy in the store. They pick them with a machine, green and not ripe, and then they let them ripen without no stem. That's why they haven't got no flavor.

6

CORN AND OTHER VEGETABLES

How to plant corn. You plant corn in rows that are 3 feet apart, so that you can walk between the rows. You make holes about 6 to 8 inches apart and 1½ to 2 inches deep, and you plant three or four seeds in each hole. After you plant them, you sprinkle them with water and keep sprinkling them until corn comes up and is 4 to 5 inches tall. Only give water if the soil is dry. Then you can stop sprinkling and start irrigating, watering the corn in the rows. Pull out any weeds that grow because they take all the energy from the soil.

When the corn gets the size of 4 or 5 or 6 inches, if all four corns in a hole comes up, pull two of them. Don't ever plant less than four, five, six or seven rows of corn. I would recommend ten rows of corn so when the corn starts to make the tassels that fall down, it germinates the corn good. Because if you put one row of corn, you never have good corn. Or even two or three rows. You have to put more than four or five. Then you'll have good ears of corn. To germinate corn, you have to have a lot of corn together.

When the corn gets the size of a foot high, you feed them. People have the idea that soil is rich. That's true, but you get a plant that has been ten years on a particular spot and all the food around is gone because the plant has been eating it. So if you want the plant to do something, you got to add some food that he likes. And you have to give something hot like rabbit or chicken manure or nitrogen. Twenty-one percent nitrogen is hot. But if you put too much, you'll burn the plants. You put a little bit at a time. You may have to feed them every week or two if it is necessary, and remember to water the rows the day before you fertilize. I must say that human manure is the best of all, but in this country it is called waste and pollution. This isn't so. In Italy we only used human manure because it is so rich in nitrogens.

For a hundred-foot row of corn, a five-gallon bucket or can of chicken or rabbit or human manure would do. You have to use your own judgment. Put the hose in the bucket and keep stirring it up and let the water and manure come out on the row. Let it go fast or one plant will get it all. I would do that especially when the plants are young so they get enough energy to give you good fruit. The younger the better, but after they grow leaves and before you transfer. This goes for all plants, not just corn. Using the water in the bucket makes it easier to not burn than if you use straight fertilizer on the plant.

Fish meal is a good source of nitrogen, but it is too expensive unless you are growing commercially. Cow and horse manure are all right if you put them in the ground and turn them in. But they're not hot enough. Not enough nitrogen. If you put fresh cow manure in the ground, don't plant for a week, but water it every day just as if you had plants in there.

Rabbit manure has 17 to 18 percent nitrogen. Also chicken

manure. Bat manure has 24 percent nitrogen, but that is too expensive. The others are cheaper and do the same work. Cow manure has about 4 percent nitrogen if it is fresh.

I would recommend after the corn get a foot or a foot and a half high, dust with sulfur like you do tomatoes, to keep away the ants. It won't kill them, but it will keep them away. And it will keep away the fungus and even other bugs that want to attack. (For more information on corn enemies, see Chapter 9.)

How do you know when the corn is ready to pick? You watch the hair. When the hair is dry and dark, that's ready to pick. If the hair is still green, it's not ready to pick. It has to stay longer in the cornstalk.

When you pick all the corn that is ripe, always leave the first corn that comes up that you think is perfect. That's for seed for next year. When you're through with the corn plant, before it gets dry, turn it under and that's your fertilizer for next year.

Now we talk about how you plant cucumbers. You plant cucumbers every 3 feet in rows that are 4 feet apart and you plant five seeds in each hole, no more than 1½ to 2 inches deep. You leave three plants in each hole and you water them just like you been doing with the other plants. Sprinkle until the plants get from 5 to 6 inches. After that, you water them in the rows. But remember this: any plant that is from 5 to 6 inches, that's when they need food. And you put the liquid food like we been talking about the other plants.

When the cucumbers grow, they make flowers. That's when you dust them with a little sulfur. I have a lot of confidence in the sulfur. It is not poison. It keeps the ants away from there. I'll tell you what the ants do, especially in cucumbers. Cucumber flowers are sweet. The ants get inside the flowers and take all the sugar that the flower has, and the plants won't make cucumbers. They will drop or make crooked cucumbers.

Bees are different. Bees take the sugar, but they will pollinate the flowers and the plant will make cucumbers. When they start to make cucumbers, if it is for cucumbers, not pickles, they got little bumps on the cucumbers. Before the bumps start to get smooth, that's ready to pick. When the cucumbers' bumps are smooth, they start to make seed and they turn from green to a lighter color. I would leave those for seed. Of course, I always leave my first perfect cucumbers for seed.

Don't ever plant cucumbers near cantaloupe or casaba or Crenshaw, because they will rob the flavor from these melons. The Crenshaw won't have any flavor at all. Or the cantaloupe. They taste more or less like cucumbers.

Now we're going to talk about how you plant broccoli and how you cut them. First, don't ever plant broccoli near cauliflowers, near kale, near collards, near mustard greens, near turnips. When you plant broccoli, they have to be absolutely by himself. I would put them not any less than 100 or 150 feet away from the things I just mentioned. If you haven't got space to put them that far, don't plant any broccoli. If you do plant broccoli near those plants, don't keep any seed because the seeds will never come true broccoli. They'll be a mixture.

If you have space and you plant broccoli (12 inches apart, in rows 3 feet apart), after the broccoli start to get 5 or 6 inches, like the other plants, you feed them with the same liquid we mentioned before. Water them in the trench. When the broccoli start to make little heads, you feed them very lightly and the heads start to get big and big and big.

How you pick broccoli? When the heads are real tight, don't pick them because they're still growing. When the heads start to release and get loose, that's the time to pick them. Now, where are you going to cut them? Don't cut them too high, because if you do, you won't have any more good broccoli coming up. This is important. You cut them three to four leaves from the bottom of the stem, so when the broccoli starts to grow they throw broccoli again and they make heads, not big like the first time, but they do make nice heads. That's on the first cut.

On the second cutting, you cut them no more than one or two leaves from the joint where the broccoli starts to branch out. Because if you cut them higher than that, the heads won't be any more than 2 inches big. But if you leave one leaf, you will have one shoot coming up and the heads will be good size.

A broccoli is good for two years. In fact, I've had cases of cutting broccoli up to three years. But you have to feed the plants to help the broccoli. Feed them regularly, every fifteen or twenty days. The way you cut them is important too. Because if you cut them too low, you won't have any more. And if you cut them too high, you'll have real small broccoli that is not fit for anything. Don't even bother to pick them.

If you're going to make seed out of the broccoli, be sure that you haven't got any wild mustard growing near there. Because if you do, you won't have a good crop of broccoli the following year.

Let's talk about how you plant celery. Celery seed is started in the flat with the compost we talked about before. When it is ready to transfer, the celery get about 4 or 5 inches high. Six inches. You get the celery from the flat, you shake the soil in the flat and separate them one by one. Then you put them in mud. Shake the roots in the mud before you plant them in the field.

Then you cut all of them 1 inch from the top of the leaves before you plant them. Then you plant them in rows 3 feet apart, on the bottom of the row if you are in a dry area like around here in Malibu. And you plant them from 6 to 8 inches apart. Again, after the plant gets from 8 to 10 inches, you feed it with the liquid fertilizer, fish or chicken or rabbit manure. Of course, with the chicken and rabbit manure, you have to make them liquid yourself by adding water.

When the celery grows to 10 inches, commercial farmers spray them with chemicals, because a lot of bugs like orange mites and black fungus attack celery. But you don't. I would put a lot of dusting sulfur, but be sure you get dusting sulfur from a nursery because dusting sulfur is not hot. They won't get any fungus.

After the celery get from six to seven leaves, you get all the leaves and tie them together. That way they get tender in the center, because otherwise the organic celery will never get tender. They'll be tough. The reason for that is that you don't feed it chemicals and they grow slowly. When they grow slowly, they get a lot of sunshine and the plant gets tough and hard. But if you tie up all the leaves together, the celery gets tenderer and sweeter.

In warm places like California, when it is the middle of September, it is time to plant in flats or boxes for wintertime vegetables. Let's start with what vegetables you're going to plant in the wintertime. You can plant cauliflower, lettuce, broccoli, kale, mustard greens, collards, radishes, onions. Most of these plants have to be started in the flats. Also, you can plant carrots, but not in the flats. Carrots have to be started in the field. Also, you can plant winter tomatoes. You start them in the flats also. But not carrots.

We talked before about how to start these plants in the flats and how to take care of them. In a month or a month and a half, the plants will be ready to transfer to the field. If you start on the fifteenth of August, it would be better yet for these particular wintertime plants in flats. About the end of

September you put them in rows in the ground like other plants.

Of course, in the wintertime, you don't give as much water like you been giving. You water when they want it. You can tell yourself when the plant is wilty or if the ground is real dry.

Now we talk about how you take care of cauliflower. When you plant cauliflower in the field, you do the same routine like you been doing with any other plant we been talking about. Plant the cauliflowers not any less than 8 inches to a foot apart in rows 3 feet apart.

Cauliflower got heads and a lot of leaves. When the cauliflower is the size of a baseball, bring together all the leaves and tie the tips with string loosely, but tight enough so the leaves won't fall. Any kind of string will do. I use flax leaves or pampas grass leaves. You do this to keep the sun from coming in and drying up the cauliflower. That's how you bleach them. Then when you want it, you cut the string. Because cauliflower won't give you more than one crop. You do the same thing to romaine lettuce and celery. If you tie them up, you keep them tender and white inside. The sun toughens. It gives nitrogen and makes them hard. They won't be as sweet if you don't let the sun in, but they will be tender. They will be good to eat.

Now, how do you pick cauliflower and when? You don't pick cauliflower until they get the size of 8 or 10 inches. They start to split in the center. That's the time to pick. Of course, if you want them to take to the market, never wait for the cauliflower to split because the stores don't want them when they split. But that's when the flavor is.

If you plant lettuce, any kind of lettuce, plant it 7 to 8 inches apart in 3-foot-apart rows. If it is regular lettuce, you let them go, water them like you're supposed to do, until they get heads. When they get heads, don't water too much any more because the heads will crack if you give too much water. But still, you have to keep them damp so they live. When the top leaves in the head start to tarnish like rust, that means they won't grow any more and it is ready to pick.

If you plant romaine lettuce and it starts to grow, when it get ten or fifteen leaves on the outside, get all the leaves and tie them up together loose, like you do with cauliflower and celery. This is important. Don't tie it up too tight. Let them loose. And romaine lettuce will get nice heads inside and the same thing: they turn tender and sweeter.

When you plant pole beans, put a stick next to them so they can climb. At first, twist them onto the pole by hand. Then they know where to go and they go by themselves.

With all the different kinds of beans, you let the first beans go, to see what size they get. When they start to get a belly, that means they've stopped growing. If you want the beans for seed or for dry beans, then leave them alone. But if you're going to use them for green beans, pick them before they start to get a belly.

Cabbage is grown the same way, and you plant the same way for the wintertime. When you see cabbage with a head on it and the top leaves in the head start to crack just a little bit, that means it's ready to pick. If they don't crack and the top leaves turn a little brown, that's ready to pick, too. But if the cabbage is dark green, it is still growing.

When you plant watermelon or cantaloupe, put the watermelon 3½ feet apart in rows 3½ feet apart, the cantaloupe 3 feet apart in rows 3 feet apart. As with any large seed, you have to put three or four seeds in each hole. If all four grow, pull out two of them. Never leave more than two growing. That goes for zucchini, squash, beans and cucumbers. Watermelon needs lots of water and level ground and, if possible, very rich soil.

If you want to pick a watermelon and you don't know if

it is ripe or green, tap it on the center. If it sounds hollow, it's ripe. If it sounds solid, it's green. Have you ever had a doctor tap your stomach with a finger? If your stomach is constipated, it sounds solid. If you go regular to the toilet, it sounds hollow. Most any doctor used to do that—I don't know about now. The same thing goes with watermelon.

Besides tapping the watermelon, if you got a good strong fingernail, you can scrape the watermelon, and if the nail doesn't sink in, it's ripe. If the fingernail sinks in here and there, the watermelon isn't ready to be picked. But the best way is tapping.

Now with cantaloupe, you let it go in the field until, when you lift it up, it comes loose from the vine. Then it is ripe. If it is not ripe, no matter how yellow it is, don't pick it because it's still green inside. It won't be sweet enough. But if you are growing commercially, pick it when it starts to turn yellow. You have to keep turning melons in the field. If you don't, the part that touches the ground won't be sweet. Turn it over every two or three days. That also keeps the sun from burning them.

If you like big zucchini, you need to save the seed from the biggest zucchini you have. When they get to be a foot or a foot and a half long, lightly stick a fingernail in the zucchini. If it goes in, pick the zucchini, but if the skin is tough, let it go to seed.

When you store anything for the winter, you can store in hay. Put them in a box, put one layer of hay and one layer of whatever it is, and then a layer of hay on top. Potato or cabbage or whatever. Anything you store, be sure not to bump or bruise, because the bumped spot will become soft and start to decay. One decay leads to another and another and another and pretty soon they're all rotten. There's a joke that one rotten potato spoils the whole sack. That's true.

But if you are careful and store with hay, if one gets rotten, the hay absorbs the wetness from the potato or squash or pumpkin or the whatever it is. Hay or sawdust keep the fruit dry and vegetables dry.

Now, we go back to tomatoes for the wintertime. When you plant winter tomatoes, you got to plant them before the end of September. In the rows, not in the flats. Then you take care like you should. When it starts to get cold and you want tomatoes in the winter, the tomatoes start to get expensive and you can't get them in the market any more for less than 45 or 50 cents a pound. But you can have your own tomatoes by covering them up in the nighttime with plastic. If you have rows, they have plastic for rows and you put it on top. And in the morning you take it off. Don't leave the tomatoes under the plastic all day. Because if you leave the plastic all day, they won't make flowers right. They drop. If you haven't got so many tomatoes, just three or four or five plants, you can put them under a big plastic bag at night. They'll give you tomatoes all along. That's if you cover them up in the wintertime or some days that are cold. And even you can get bell peppers the same way. If it is cold, cover them up. If it is a warm and sunny day, take off the plastic. And you don't have to depend on anyone to get your tomatoes or bell peppers.

Now, any other of these winter plants don't have to be covered because they like it cold and damp and windy. That won't matter. Of course, we're not talking about where the weather freezes hard. We're talking about like in California, where they never get killed by frost. If they get a little frost, it won't matter. They'll like it. That's for wintertime plants. But don't ever plant beans, because beans are very sensitive. They won't stand any cold weather at all. String beans, squash, melon—cantaloupe, casaba, Crenshaw. Any of them plants won't take cold. Don't ever try because they won't make.

The winter plants have to have better care than summer

plants. If the rows are flat and it rains, the water will sit there and won't go away. You have to open it up so the water can get out. Don't let the water stay in the rows, sitting for two or three hours, because you'll drown them. But no matter how much it rains—it can rain three or four or five days—if the water runs out from the rows, don't worry about it. The plants will take care of themselves.

Or you can plant the wintertime plants on top of the rows. When it rains, the water runs out and the plant won't drown himself. When they are on top of the row, you have to give them better care. You have to watch them close, especially when the weather is dry. When the weather is wet, it won't matter, but you have to take care of all plants yourself, except if it is a wild plant. You have to feed them, just like you do you. You need food; they need it too. Even if your soil is pretty rich, they still need a little change. Then you see in six or seven days the difference in how the plants are doing. They change color, they stand straight up, they can stand weather better, they be strong and you have a good crop.

7

UNDERGROUND PLANTS

What we are going to talk about now is all the plants that must grow underground, like sweet potatoes, carrots, parsnips, Jerusalem artichokes, turnips.

Let's take sweet potatoes, for instance. Let's begin with how we going to plant them. The best way is to get a sweet potato and a glass of water. You can start them in the kitchen.

Fill up a glass of water and put the root end of the sweet potato in the water and let it sprout in the kitchen or any place that is warm. I usually use a clay bowl or get a regular clay pot and plug the hole. Fill it up full of water. I put three or four or five sweet potatoes in there. And I make sure that they always have water in the pot. In an 8-inch pot I have six to ten potatoes. When they start to sprout, they have little shoots, and them shoots have roots. You pull them off, roots and all, and you've got your sweet potato plant. I've picked up to twelve little shoots out of one potato.

After I pull the new shoots and roots off the potato, I immediately put them in another glass with water so they don't suffer. And you can use the sweet potato that is left over for eating.

Now we prepare the soil. I usually pick where it is pretty loamy, sandy soil. They like sandy soil. I have a tractor now, but when I didn't I turned the soil with a fork, about a foot or a foot and a half deep. First I put a lot of hay or horse manure on top of the soil. Anything that makes the soil loose. They like the soil loose because they got to travel under the soil. If the soil is hard you'll get little stubby potatoes that won't be good-sized or good tasting.

After I have 3 or 4 inches of hay or straw on the soil, I turn the soil upside down. I do that before I plant the potatoes in the pot. And let the soil rest while the potatoes are in the water. Then, when they start to shoot, I go back to the soil and turn it over again. And I make rows about 3 feet apart and make sure the trenches are 2 feet wide. This is for the West Coast. Don't make the rows so slopey that, when you put the water at one end, in one minute you've got it at the other end. Be sure the soil is level as possible, but not too level. The water has to run out. If it is perfectly level the water will stand and get sour and that's bad for the plants. The water has to go slowly and the soil stay damp. My soil has a half an inch to an inch of slope for each foot. But no more.

After you have the soil ready and the shoots with the little roots in a glass of water away from the mother, you go out and plant them. Plant them 3 to 5 feet apart and 3 inches deep. If you are in a damp, humid place, like Cheyenne, Wyoming, or Oregon or the East Coast, put them on top of the rows. But still, the rows have to be 3 feet apart. If you are in a dry place with little rain, put them in the trenches, so when you water the plants, they'll get the water.

Plant them 3 to 5 feet apart in the row, because sweet potatoes like to travel. I've seen them travel 5 or 6 feet. If you put them on top of the hill, on top of the trench, be sure that when they throw little sweet potatoes, you cover them up with soil. Don't ever leave them uncovered because they will turn green and lose their taste. That's for sweet potatoes.

Now, for regular potatoes, Irish potatoes, red potatoes, russet potatoes, you get the potatoes that have a lot of eyes. For instance, if you get a potato that is 3 inches round and 5 or 6 inches long, you should find five or six eyes to make potatoes from. I've made up to eight from one mother. Never use a potato less than 1 inch wide and 2 inches long because if the mother is small, the shoots will come real skinny. Until they start to grow, potatoes feed themselves from the mother. After they have their own roots, they don't need the mother any more. They take care of themselves when they have a lot of roots.

When they are ready to plant, you cut up the potato, leaving an eye with root in each piece. And the same as with sweet potatoes, if it is a dry place, plant them in the gully, 3 inches deep, and if it is damp, plant them on top of the trenches. And also I wouldn't put regular potatoes less than a foot apart, and I keep the rows 3 or 4 feet apart.

With Jerusalem artichokes, you work the ground just like with the sweet potatoes. With all these root plants that grow underground, the soil has to be absolutely loose. If it is hard soil, like adobe or clay, you never get good-formed potatoes, turnips, carrots or whatever. It has to be soft so the roots can travel.

I use Jerusalem artichokes that have a lot of knots because that means they have a lot of eyes. I wouldn't cut the Jerusalem artichokes because they get moldy. You can cut them and dry them, but if you don't know what you're doing, I wouldn't monkey with it. So I break the knots off the Jerusalem artichokes and put them aside for seed. And you eat the Jerusalem artichoke itself. Then, when planting time comes, I make soil just for like sweet potatoes and plant them just like sweet potatoes. I usually plant them in January, but if you are on the East Coast, you take a big chance planting after the frost because the frost may come back. You have to use your own judgment. Water them when you plant them and then let them go. When they start to shoot, water them again. I wouldn't water them too much. The same goes for the potatoes. If the soil is damp, that's plenty.

How do you know when the sweet potatoes are ready for picking? Sweet potatoes usually throw a little pinkish-purple flower. After the flower is gone, you have sweet potatoes under.

With Irish potatoes, you wait until the plants start to dry out. Don't pull them before that. After the plant is half dead, half dried out, dig it out and you'll have nice-sized potatoes, already formed and good tasting. A lot of potatoes are always sweet because I pick them at the right time. If you wait until the plant is completely dead, the potatoes will still be good, but they haven't got the flavor. If you pick the potatoes before the plant starts to die, the potato is still good, but it isn't mature enough to have the flavor. But if you pick when I say, the potatoes will be sweet and tasty.

Then you store them in the coolest, driest place you have. When I haven't got a cool spot, I dig a hole in the ground, put in some hay, put the potatoes on top of the hay and more hay on top of the potatoes and then soil on top. Then when I want some potatoes, I go and dig them out. That's if I have too many potatoes, because in a cool place they're good for a month or a month and a half or more after you pick them. They stay even longer in the ground than if you pick them and store them.

Jerusalem artichokes make little flowers like the little sunflower that grows wild. When the flower is through blooming and starts to wilt, underground the Jerusalem artichokes are

starting to form. I don't know where we get the name Jerusalem artichokes because they are like potatoes, but that's what
we call them.

With Jerusalem artichokes, just like with potatoes, if they
show above ground, cover them up with soil. When the
flowers are all finished, the Jerusalem artichokes are still
growing. Don't pick them until the trunk from the stem is
dry. Then you have all the energy from the plant in the
Jerusalem artichokes. That's the time to pick them. I pick
them whenever I need them until they start to sprout. I leave
them in the ground until spring. Then I pull them all out
and put them in the icebox. If you have room in the icebox
and you put the Jerusalem artichokes in a plastic bag, they'll
be good for three or four months without losing anything. And
that's the way I do Jerusalem artichokes.

Now if you are going to plant turnips, you make your soil
just like we been talking about and you make the patch very
level. The way I do that is to get a long board and put one
guy at each end and keep going back and forth. When the
planting place is level, you get some turnip seed and put one
package in an empty one-gallon can with half a gallon sand.
Mix it very well with the seeds. Take the can to the ready
soil, take a handful of sand and seed and throw it as far as
you can. The reason for that is that the seeds won't fall down
one on top of the other. That's called broadcasting the seeds.
They'll be all even. Or you can make rows 3 feet apart.

Don't turn the ground over after broadcasting the seeds,
because if you put too much ground on top of the seeds, the
turnips won't make very big heads. Sprinkle no more than ½
inch of soil on top of the turnip seeds. Quarter inch is better.
Then sprinkle with water. We do this with turnips, kohlrabi
and rutabagas, but not with carrots.

For carrots you fix your soil the same as with the sweet
potatoes; it has to be loose and deeply turned over. You

level the ground just like with turnips and mix the seeds in sand so you can broadcast them good all over the patch or in the rows. You throw your seeds and then get a hoe and turn it over. But not too deep. About an inch or an inch and a half. Maybe 2 inches would be all right too. But not any deeper. Then water them. Sprinkle light.

Now with all these plants that you broadcast, like turnips, parsnips, rutabagas, carrots, after you plant the seeds you have to water daily, especially in summertime. Every morning sprinkle with water lightly, but give enough that they can start to grow. If you don't do that, the little germ will start to grow and the sun will hit it, especially if it is a hot sun and the ground is dry, and the germ will dry out and die. Sprinkle every morning without fail until the plants have three leaves. After that you can water every second day, then every third day until you water every week or less depending how the weather is.

Now how do you know when to start to pick beets, kohlrabi, turnips, parsnips or rutabagas? When there are about eight to ten leaves, you open up the leaves and see if the heads are sticking out of the ground. That's why I want you to plant them so close to the top of the ground. You can tell without digging out if it is big enough to use or not. I usually let them get big enough so that I can have a meal out of two or three turnips or parsnips or like that.

Carrots are different. Carrots you can tell by after they got eight or ten or twelve leaves, the leaves start to bush out. But if the leaves are still flat on the ground, the carrots are still growing. Or you dig out a little and see what size carrots you got. And you pull them out with a fork because if you try to pull out with your hands, you'll have the leaves in the hand and the carrots will stay in the soil.

One thing you have to remember that's very important about sweet potatoes, Irish potatoes and Jerusalem artichokes

is that the gophers really love them. You have to watch for
the gophers and moles. When you see a mound of fresh soil,
there's a gopher under there. And believe me, one gopher
won't let you have any potatoes or Jerusalem artichokes. There
are a lot of ways to kill gophers. One way, if you are near
a road, is to run a big hose from a car exhaust to the hole.
Let the car run for about an hour. If it is a fresh hole, chances
are you will kill him. But he might go out from another door
because every fifteen or twenty feet they have an outlet. I've
seen tunnels that run over a mile and a half. Then you can't
kill him with the fumes.

Or if the hole is fresh, you can fill it up with water and
when he comes out, you be ready with a stick or a club to
hit him on the head. Because either eliminate him or you
don't eat the potatoes or the turnips.

Another way you can control them if they have a highway
under there is to find the tunnel by digging with a shovel or
a fork. When you find the tunnel, pack it with broken glass
like from a milk bottle or gallon jug. But put it deep enough
so you don't cut yourself when you work there again because
glass never decays. Of course, if you get a smart gopher, he'll
go to another place and make a connecting tunnel. That's
happened to me. But if he cuts his paw when he's digging,
he'll go far away because he knows it's dangerous. That way
you control a little bit. But you have to be persistent like he
is. Whoever is more persistent, you or him, gets the food.

Now we have another thing that grows under the ground.
That's peanuts. But peanuts are a little different. The way
you get your seed is to find raw unroasted peanuts in the
shell that haven't been fumigated, because when they fumigate, they kill the germ and the peanuts never grow. How can
you tell if the peanuts are good or not? I buy my peanuts from
the big feed store. Shell your peanuts and spread them. You
usually can tell if the germ inside the peanut is alive or dead.

If the germ is very sharp looking and green, that means it's alive. If the germ is a little brown and dried up, don't bother to plant it because it won't grow.

To plant peanuts, prepare the soil like you did with sweet potatoes. Then make a hole about a foot around and 6 to 8 inches deep and put a little mound of soil in the center of the hole and put about three shelled peanuts. Cover them up, but don't water them right away or they will rot. After they start growing, you water them regularly. Usually when it is full grown you keep on adding soil on top of the trench until the plant starts to wilt. When the plant starts to wilt, you dig it out a little bit and you see the peanuts starting to come out of there. Sometimes I pick up all the peanuts, but leave the little ones and cover them up again because there is a chance that I will have peanuts until the end of the season. I've found places where the peanuts grow the next year out of the same plant.

All the plants that grow underground have to be planted in the dark of the moon, after the full moon. This is very important; otherwise you won't have a good crop. The best time is during the first fertile sign after the full moon. (See Gardening by the Moon at the back of this book.)

8

ARTICHOKES

Now how do you plant artichokes, how you thin them down, and what to do when the artichokes start growing?

What are we going to plant to make artichokes? You get a sucker that is growing on the side of the artichoke plant. Be sure the sucker you get from the mother plant has little roots. Don't pull it out from the mother plant. Make a hole all the way around the mother. Take away all the soil and then you'll see the ones that have roots. And cut them pretty close to the mother. Usually they have one or two roots on the little suckers. That's the ones you plant. Cut all the leaves from the sucker except the center leaves and leave 6 to 8 inches from the roots up. Don't cover the leaves that are on the center of the sucker. These leaves have to be out of the ground because, if you do cover them with the ground, the plant can't breathe and it will die. The only way the plant can breathe is with the leaves.

If you don't have an artichoke plant, check with a local

nursery to find out when artichoke season starts so you can buy some from them. Plant no less than half a dozen. If they don't have any, send me 75 cents per plant and postage and I will send you some. Write to Chico, 30040 Morning View Drive, Malibu, California, 90265.

To plant, I make a hole 3 feet wide and about 3 feet deep. Then I partly fill with 2 feet of good, loose, mixed soil. I mix peat moss, leaf mold, sandy soil and a little adobe. Then I set the suckers on top, 1 foot apart, and add another 6 inches of soil around the plants. Make sure that you cover the roots, but not the leaves. If you got a hole 3 feet wide, I would put four artichoke suckers all the way around and one in the center.

But I still leave a circular trench in the hole that I made so I can water it. And I water it good. Also, I put a couple handsful of bone meal before I water. Then I give them a good soaking of water and I water them every week. That's for around here where I am in Malibu, because it's a real dry place. But if it is any place that has a lot of rain or moisture, you don't have to water them every week.

But no matter where you are, just after you plant them, I would water. The simple reason for that is so the water packs the soil around the little roots that are first starting when you transfer from the mother plant. That's why I want you to water them when you plant them.

You keep watering until they start new leaves. After they start new leaves, and the new leaves are about 5 or 6 inches high from the ground, you feed them. Feed them in the trench and don't let it touch the artichokes. When you feed them, you mix some blood meal and bone meal. That's when it is 6 inches high. From there on they will bush out and grow fast. When they get about a foot or a foot and a half high, then you feed real strong fertilizer. The strongest fertilizer you can get. What I would feed is strong fish meal, liquid fish

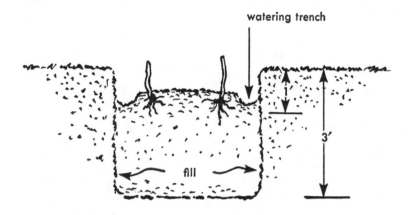

watering trench

fill

3'

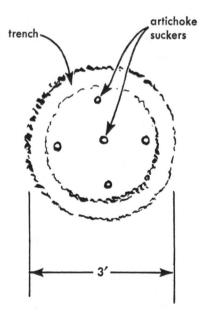

trench

artichoke
suckers

3'

Planting Artichokes

fertilizer. The higher the nitrogen you give to the artichokes, the better it is. I usually get 21 or 22 percent nitrogen for the artichokes. Then you get real big artichokes.

From then on, about two or three weeks after you feed them, you see little buds in the center of the artichoke plant. Watch for the buds to come out. When they get a little bigger than a marble, you give another feed. You feed them good again. Then don't feed them any more.

Usually they make three to five artichokes on each stem. That's the center stem. When the artichokes from the mother stem are all gone, you can give another feeding. Then you get artichokes on the suckers around the mother.

I'd like to mention this: when the artichokes start growing and they get a nice-sized bush, you have to take off all the old leaves that are on the bottom of the stem in the trench. The simple reason for that is so the bugs won't hide themselves under there. Also, the roots don't have to feed all them excess leaves. If you leave them, the artichokes will come out small. When you take the leaves off, the artichokes come nice and big and they make a lot of artichokes.

I'm going to give you a small example. I had a few students that lived on my place. And they had a beautiful cat. This cat had six babies and I told the students, "Take some of the babies out because they going to kill the cat."

They didn't want to do that because they feel bad taking the baby away from the mother. So they didn't. Those six babies drained the poor mother cat until the mother got skinny like a bone and didn't even have ambitions to eat. And it did kill the mother, because a mother always, no matter what happens to her, she will take care of the baby. And she die herself so the baby keeps on living. And that's the way the plant is. That's the way the artichokes will be if you don't take all the old excess leaves that are no good to her and no good to you.

Artichokes get black aphids, green aphids and fungus, and they will cripple the artichokes. You have to give strong sulfur. I mix sulfur, white ashes, raw lime and bone meal. You won't kill them, but you will discourage them if you dust them with that. The sulfur will discourage the fungus, the ashes will discourage the mealy bugs and the bone meal and the lime will discourage the aphids.

We have another enemy of the artichokes: the little butterfly that has wings like an airplane. It's a small one. Very pretty and spotted. That's the worst enemy we have with the artichokes. They lay eggs inside the artichoke when it is real small and then the little moths, like maggots, go into the heart of the artichoke and they keep eating the inside of the artichoke, but you can't see them. There's nothing you can do about it. I never been able to find anything to do about that. But if you see one of them, pick it and destroy it. Burn him or put him inside a bottle and put the cork tight so it won't come out. When you do that, you control most of the moths and the little flies that come out. Them moths, even when the artichokes are all gone, they go inside the trunk and on the first leaves that start to come out, they go inside, and from there on they feed themselves from the artichokes.

Also, when the leaves are all gone, the moth knows she hasn't got any more food and she preserves herself until spring. She makes a hard shell coat on the outside, so she won't suffer from the cold, the rain or the lack of food. Then, the first rain, the dampness and the water softens down the shell she made before winter and she comes out again. She comes out and goes back to the artichokes like last year. As soon as the artichokes come out, she goes to the center and starts to eat the artichokes again.

Each artichoke bush, the mother stem usually makes four or five artichokes. When the stem is through making artichokes, be sure to take the stem off from the bottom of the roots, because if there is any disease on the stem, the bugs carry it on to the next stem. They go on the new sucker and start to feed on it. You take that one out and put it on a place where you can burn it. Because that's about the worst enemy we have on artichokes: the bugs that go inside and there's nothing you can do about it. Aphids you can usually wash down, by sprinkling water, but you can't wash away the moths that get inside the artichokes.

9

INSECTS AND DISEASE

Now we're going to talk about how you know if the plants have insects or disease and what to look for.

Each kind of tree has different kinds of disease and different kinds of bugs. Let's say lemon trees. Lemon trees have mealy bugs, scales and lice. How can you know that by looking at the tree? You see white spots, usually on the inside, on the thick branches, thicker than a finger. Little white lumps. That's mealy bugs. Then sometimes they have black scales, and the way to tell is that some of the ¼-inch-thick branches have little black lumps all the way around. I usually get a knife or something to lift up the lump and see how it is inside. If it's yellow inside, the bugs are still alive. Also, they have what we call *pidocchio*, or lice, that's little black spots right on the lemon. Not on the trunk or leaves, but on the lemon itself. The lemon won't look so good and that's no good for market.

Now, what to do if the tree has bugs. Scales have to be

sprayed with anything that contains oil. I usually take equal parts of mineral oil and liquid sulfur and nondetergent soap and make a spray out of it. I spray all the trunk and all the leaves three times, two weeks apart. That usually controls the scales and sometimes the mealy bugs. But don't put any more than three tablespoons of the mixture you make for each gallon of water.

Another way you can tell if the tree has disease is when you see ants going up and down the trunk. Follow the ants, and at the end you'll find disease. You usually find mealy bugs or scales on the lemon tree. Also, they will get what we call dry rot. How can you tell that? Somewhere on the branches or trunk, a little gum sticks out. When you see the gum on a lemon tree there is very serious danger. You spray with anything that contains copper. And you give three sprays. Or, if it is a small branch, cut it off and burn it. Also do that if there is just one branch that has scales or mealy bugs.

Oranges get the same kind of diseases, and also aphids when they have young leaves. Again you can tell when the ants go up and down and when you see the tips of young leaves curl in. Look under the leaves and nine out of ten you'll find aphids or little green worms. How do you spray for that if you are organic? For aphids you get nondetergent soap, natural soap. You make a liquid out of it and you spray. Not too strong, though. A couple tablespoons to a gallon of water. If that won't do, mix some mineral oil with the soap before you put it in the water. Put enough soap so the oil turns white. Then you put it in water. Also you can add one tablespoon liquid pure sulfur per gallon.

If it is for scales, the spray has to be stronger because scales breathe from the top and you have to seal it so they can't breathe. For that you mix equal parts of nondetergent soap, liquid sulfur and mineral oil and add three tablespoons to a gallon of water. Always mix the oil and the soap first, then add the other things and the water. If you want to make this mixture better yet, after you have mixed it all in a gallon water, add three tablespoons of raw lime (hot lime), one tablespoon wood ashes and one tablespoon bone meal. That's for the oranges or any other plants that have disease, except if the plants are real tender.

Now, how can you tell if a peach tree has bugs? You look at the leaves, especially when they're young. The end of the leaves roll under. That's what we call leaf miner or leaf curl. You can't do nothing about that as long as the peach tree— or almond or nectarine or apricot or apple or pear—has leaves. Another way you can tell is when the trunk of one of these trees has gum coming out of the tree. That means there's bugs in there. But there's nothing you can do about it until the tree drops all the leaves. After that happens, you spray the trunk and branches three or four times with the same mixture you did before for the lemon trees.

You got to remember this: if a tree has leaf miner you have to add a little liquid copper or a little liquid sulfur. Not all nurseries carry liquid copper and liquid sulfur. You have to go to a reliable nursery. What the bug does is after the leaves are gone and he hasn't got any more food, he goes inside the trunk and preserves himself and nobody can get him until it is spring again and after the rains. He comes out of the trunk and that's where the gum comes from. Because he's been there and the tree start to cry and form a gum.

The same thing with walnut trees. But the walnut tree has a little different bug than the peach tree. With the peach tree it is very seldom that the bug attacks the peach, but they will attack the tree and leaves. But the one on the walnut tree will attack the walnuts before the walnuts get hard. When the shell starts to open, he goes inside the walnuts and eats all the walnuts. That's the bug that goes back into the trunk. To stop that you have to do the same as peaches. And you will stop them.

Avocado. They usually get scales. First the scales start on the trunk. From the trunk they go to the stem of the avocado and they suck all the juice from the stem. When they have too much scales, the avocados drop down before they are full-grown. Sometimes the tree has a lot of energy and supports both the avocado and the scales. But if it is for commercial crop, it don't look good and people think it's bad. They don't know that that's how you know if the avocado is organic or not. They look bad and they won't buy them. So you have to spray with the same formula as before. Of course the avocado is very hard to spray. You have to go under the tree, in the leaves, and spray from the inside out. Otherwise you'll never get them because avocados stay under the leaves. But if you do that, you'll control most of the bugs.

What I would do first is wash them with strong pressure water, to get rid of the mother. Then let them dry and then spray. And get some lime in a bucket, put in some water and make lime wash and paint a ring of lime around the trunk, and sometimes you discourage the ants from going up and down. Ants are about the worst enemy we have, because they carry a lot of bugs and disease from one place to another.

Sometimes you see people put sticky flypaper to stop the ants, but they get old in two or three days and it's not so good. The best way is whenever you see a hole in the ground with ants going in and out, you put sulfur and destroy them.

Now for vegetables. With tomatoes, for instance, how do you know if they have the big bugs without seeing them? If the tomatoes aren't staked, lift them off the ground whenever you pass by or whenever you water. If you see black round drops, that means the big bug with the horns—the zebra swallowtail—is in there. If you don't have so many tomatoes, whenever you see the bug, destroy him. But whenever you see one bug with horns, if you look around you'll find another. They always travel in pairs. If you have a lot of tomatoes, you have to spray with the same formula just like with trees. It is very seldom that tomatoes get aphids.

Spinach and swiss chard get aphids. Celery gets aphids and black fungus and mites. Celery is about the worst at collecting insects. But if you spray with the same mixture you'll control the insects on most any plant.

On the spinach you look for curled-up leaves. You lift the leaf up and you'll find bugs underneath.

Broccoli is very susceptible to aphids. That's why it's hard to find broccoli that is organic. Because it's a lot of work. The aphids start when the broccoli make little heads. The aphids get in and start to propagate. Pretty soon all the heads are full of aphids. What I do is I get a hose with a lot of pressure and wash them. Then I spray with the same mixture as for the trees. It controls some, but not much. About 75 percent. That's for broccoli.

Cabbage. You can tell if cabbage has bugs by lifting up a leaf and inside the leaf it's dark. Usually you see a lot of bug droppings in there even if you don't see the bugs. They're in there. In the daytime they come out of the center and go on the tips of the leaves under the leaf and eat there all day. Then in the night they go in the center because the center is pretty warm. And they leave droppings before they come out. They do that with cabbage and cauliflower.

Now the cauliflowers have little green worms that go inside the cauliflower and inside the leaves. And cauliflowers get aphids too. Lots of aphids. But you can control with the same mixture you made for the peaches and the lemon. But first you have to wash them with water. And I would spray not any less than once a week. Then you control most any kind of pest that goes to your plants. Watch them all the time, looking for the bugs. Sometimes you can tell if there are holes in the leaves. You can depend that there's a bug in there even if you don't see the bug. And I won't stop looking until I see the bug, and then I do what I have to do.

Of course we have a bug that there's nothing we can do about it. That's nematode. Nematode you usually find in sandy soil. They go in the roots of the plant and cripple the roots. Now how can you tell that? Nematode gets in the roots and forms a ball. If you see a plant that has something wrong, the leaves turn yellow and start to die, don't give up. Take a look and see what's the matter with the plant. If you can't see nothing on top of the roots, take the plant out carefully and see what's the matter with the roots. If it has nematode there will be little balls in the roots. When you see that, pull up the plant, roots and all, and burn it. If you have nematode on one plant, you can be sure they will go to the other plants. And so far I never find any solution for nematode in the soil. There is a solution by fumigating, but if you fumigate and you have a small yard, that's all right, but who's going to fumigate your neighbor? And if you have a big farm, how can you fumigate the whole farm? However, there are certain plants that get along with nematodes, mostly shallow-rooted plants, and you can plant them. Otherwise, there are two things you can do: move or don't plant.

Vegetables in the ground, like carrots, turnips, parsnips, get slugs and sour bugs and a little beetle that goes underground. That's what damages plants that grow underground. Now what to do to control that? Before I start to plant, I put a lot of dusting sulfur or ground sulfur on the ground and turn it under. (Or hot lime, gypsum, anything like that they don't like.) And also I delay my watering a little bit until the sulfur controls most of the pests. It won't kill them, but it controls them. Because when you delay your water, they don't have enough dampness because any bugs that attack underground vegetables like a lot of moisture. And if you haven't got much moisture, they won't live in there. They go where the moisture is, even if they are hungry. They make a hole in the carrots and they get rotten. The same with the parsnips. There's not much you can do except put the sulfur before you plant them. The same with the parsnips. By the time you pick your crop, the bug won't go there. A little, but not too much.

Now we talk about the bugs that go to the corn. The green worm, the brown worm, all different kinds of worms, are from the pretty little butterfly that flies around. She never misses any corn and she's the one that lays the egg on top of the silk and that egg starts to grow on the very tender silk and starts to go down. They grow together, the silk, the corncob and the worm. They grow at the same time. As the corn gets bigger, the bug gets bigger. What can you do there, because there is no way you can see the bug that is inside the corn?

You can keep the butterfly from laying eggs on the corn. You get an eyedropper and you put 3 parts castor oil and 1 part mineral oil. When the silk just about comes out from the corncob, when it is really young, before the tassel comes up from the cornstalk, you put one or two drops of oil on the tassel. That's the first treatment. Then when the corn starts to make silk, you put two or three drops inside the silk on each corn. Usually one stalk has three or four corns.

When the butterfly drops the eggs on there, if she's not in a hurry, she sees or smells the castor oil and keeps on moving. But sometimes she's in a hurry and she drops the egg in the hair and the hair got castor oil and the egg never germinates. It will die. See, the butterfly lays so many eggs that it is pitiful. Two butterflies got enough eggs to supply two acres of corn. And each corncob gets one or two eggs. It's a lot of work to put the castor oil. I know because I had three acres of corn once and I had to put castor oil on each one. And believe me, the ones I missed with the castor oil, she didn't miss with the eggs, because she visits each stalk, back and forth, back and forth, and you have to do this sometimes three times through the corn season. Maybe you get away with two times, but then at the end you have bugs. Especially if you want to make seed out of the corn.

The way you make seed is you put a tag with the date on the first cornstalk that comes out and that will be your seed. You never pick that one. But be sure to put oil on it. Let it grow. I usually leave all three or four corncobs that the stalk has. I leave them until the stalk gets completely dry. Then I take it up, stalk and all, and hang them to let them dry. The reason for that is that the seeds get all the energy from the mother, and when you plant them you'll have good husky corn because he was husky before you plant him. That's the reason the plant has corn before the others. I've had three acres of corn and I've taken care of them exactly the same, but one stalk will come out two weeks before the others. The reason is unknown. It is like the same mother and father have six children and care for them the same, but one grows to be six feet and all the others only four or five.

Now the bugs that go on the grapes are fungus and little mites. They go in the bunches of grapes when they are in bloom, and usually you can tell when little tiny grapes fall to the ground. That means something is wrong with the plant. The little mites eat the stem and suck the juice and let it drop down. What you do is you get straight dusting sulfur, nothing else, get a dusting gun and be sure you dust all the way around, under and on the top lightly. I usually dust the grapes three times; when the grapes is in bloom and when the grapes start and when they get the size of a marble. You do two things: you kill the germs and you help the plant to grow. No ants go around there and no fungus on the grapes. That's what I do for the grapes.

10

APRICOTS, MULBERRIES
AND POMEGRANATES

Now we talk a little bit about apricots, because apricots are very good for anybody that has trouble with the blood. Out of the apricots you can eat the fruit fresh, or you can dry them and eat them whenever you want to.

How you dry them. You get the apricots when they're dead ripe. You cut them in half and take the seed out. But don't throw out the seed because it's the best. Split the apricots in half and put them on a screen, about 2 or 3 inches above the ground or above a table. What I do, if the apricots are real sweet, I don't add nothing. Then, on top of the screen I put the apricots, and on top of the apricots I put a screen or curtain so the flies and insects won't go there.

If the apricots are not sweet, I sprinkle a little raw sugar on top of the apricots and let them dry together. But be sure to put a screen or old curtain on top. Otherwise you'll have a lot of bugs and flies. The flies carry the worst germs that anybody ever had. Any insect that flies from one place to another carries germs and disease.

Be sure that you put the apricots out in the morning and bring them in at night. Because if you don't, even if there is no dew or fog, if the daytime is hot and the nighttime cold, they get damp and they will mold and get rotten. But if you bring them in at sundown and put them out at sunup you will have nice dry apricots. And you store them in plastic or cellophane bags so they keep moist and never dry real hard like if you put them any place else.

Now we go back to the pit. You crack the pit with a hammer. (Of course I crack mine with my teeth, and I'm seventy-two years old.) Take the inside of the pit (the seed or kernel). If you want to store them, let them dry completely. Spread them out on a table or piece of board. They shouldn't touch each other. When they are completely dry, store them in a plastic bag or inside a jar.

What do you do with the seed? First you can make the best drink for a hot day. Nothing better than that. If you have a blender, put about 10 or 15 seeds inside the blender with 3 cups of water and about 3 tablespoons sugar or honey. Blend them, put in some ice and that's the best drink you ever had.

If you want to use it as medicine, with the seed from apricots, you can cure many illnesses, some say even cancer. That's how good they are. Of course you make it a little stronger. Instead of 15, put 25 or 30 seeds. If you don't want to take them as a drink, grind them and take as a tea. If you don't want to take as a tea, grind them and dry and put them in capsules and take three capsules a day. If you drink three or four cups of apricot-seed tea a day you'll be healthy. Use the inside from apricot seeds, not the hard outside.

The seed from apricots is the most important tea that we have. Nothing better than that. You can get seeds from peaches, but it's nothing like apricots.

And I use it all the time. In fact when I was eight years old, that was my first business. Me and my brother. Sixty-four years ago. That's how I know about seeds from apricots. We used to go to market, buy apricots, get the seeds, put them inside a sack and squash them with a hammer. Then we put sugar in there and we made a drink. The color of the drink is white like milk. We used to stand on the street corner with a box and the drink and glasses on top of the box and we used to sell it two glasses for a penny. That's how I used to make my spending money. Me and my brother. Whoever bought once, they came back and bought more drink. They didn't know what the heck it was, but it tasted so good. Not kids, I'm talking about grown-up people. We used to sell it just as fast as we made it.

Then my father saw that we had a good business and he went to market and he bought boxes of apricots. My mother used to make a jam and we used to take the seeds to make a drink. And my mother didn't have to tell me two times, "Chico, go open the apricots so I can make jam," because that was my money. I was glad to help my mother make apricot jam. And we used to eat the jam in the wintertime, and I used to store the seeds just like I said. That's how much I know about apricots.

Now we going to talk about mulberry trees. Most people don't know what a mulberry is. We have four kinds of mulberry. One gets silkworm that makes silk out of it. They make little mulberries, not much fit to eat. Another one makes little white mulberries, and the silkworm will attack that too. You can eat that, but there's not much flavor to it. Not sweet enough. Then we have little purple-pink mulberries. They're long, about the size of the joint on the tip of your little finger. You can eat that too. It's a little sweeter than the other one. Then we have a little blue-purple mulberry that is a little bigger than the others. That's the best American mulberry to eat.

Then we have what I call Italian mulberry. It is as big as the first joint of your thumb and long, in fact it's bigger than a boysenberry. Some of them are as much as an inch long. And a few mulberries make a darn good breakfast dish. That's about the best mulberry. The flavor is out of this world. And if you have any disease in your mouth, any sore mouth or gums, any bad teeth, we make a syrup out of the mulberry for it and use it as a mouth tonic. They're very good, no matter what you have in your mouth. Even if your teeth are weak, they'll make your teeth strong. If your gums are sore, they'll heal it up. Nothing better than mulberries to take care of the mouth. I also make a hair tonic from mulberries.

Out of Italian mulberry, you can get the leaves, dry them, crush them and make tea to drink for rinsing out your mouth. Especially if you have a child and you want your child to get strong teeth, you give mulberry-leaf tea. Or you can make tea from the bark of the roots of the mulberry tree. And your teeth will always be good.

I been wondering why I have such good teeth. I'm seventy-two years old and I have all my teeth and all my hair. I like Italian mulberry. I go crazy every year and I eat a lot of them. I guess that's why my teeth are so good.

Also you can get fig leaves. Dry them and grind them if you have a blender. If you haven't got a blender, crush them with your hands. You get them in the summertime and after they are dried and crushed, you store them in a plastic bag. Fig-leaf tea is very good for your stomach.

And grape leaves are useful, especially when you get the tips when they are very young. You dry them, crush them or grind them and make a tea. Nothing better than these three trees to take care of most anything in your body: mulberry-leaf tea for the mouth, fig-leaf tea for your stomach, and grape leaves for the blood and liver.

If you have any kind of boil or pimple that throws pus, get the leaves from boysenberries when the leaves are still green. Try to get perfect leaves. Open up the boil or pimple a little bit on the tip and put the leaves smooth side down on the boil. Stretch the leaves out and put three or four on top of the boil and tie them up. Them leaves draw all the pus out of the boil.

If you have trouble with your mouth, get the roots from the mulberry and the bark from the roots of the pomegranate. Dry them, grind them and make a tea. If you drink about five cups of that tea a day, you won't have any fistula or any piles. You can even cure colitis. If you haven't got the roots from the pomegranate tree, you can use the skin from the pomegranate or the flowers. Or you can use the leaves. All are good, but the bark from the roots is best. But if you don't want to damage your tree, you can use the skin from the fruit, the leaves and the flowers. The male flowers, not the female.

How do you know which is which? On the back of the flowers, where the stem comes up, the female flowers have a little ball. The one that has a little stub instead of a ball, that's the male. If you haven't got pomegranates in your yard, find out who does. Usually the male flowers, when they're full grown, drop down. Ask the owner if you can pick up the flowers from the ground. He'll be glad to let you have them because he doesn't have no use for them. And that's very good for colitis, fistula or piles.

If you have piles on the outside, get the leaves or bark from the pomegranate, make a strong tea and bathe them with a piece of cotton three or four times a day. Then you leave the cotton wet on the piles if you can. That's the best medicine for piles.

11

FIGS

Now about figs. We are in the first part of January, and that's the best time to prune fig trees and get suckers for planting.

Usually, fig trees have a tendency to start growing from the side of the trunk, on the roots. We call these suckers. Every year, you take them off and cut them very close to the roots and trunk. If you have any suckers, that's your start for a new tree. That is what you plant to make another tree. If you haven't got any roots, take the lowest sucker on the trunk, whether it has roots or not. You plant it and it will grow. Plant it about a foot deep or a foot and a half, and leave 6 or 7 inches out of the ground. And cut the bottom tips off the suckers when you plant them. Be sure that the end that goes in the ground is cut real sharp. Get a sharp knife or an old-fashioned razor. If you don't do that, the end of the branch will get moldy when you water it, and it will rot and never have a chance to start growing. But if it is clean cut, without any bruises on the end, it will grow.

Of course, if it don't rain any more, you have to water. At least once a week until it starts to grow, and in the spring it will start to shoot. If it throws more than one shoot on the side, take them off and leave only one shoot to go straight up. That's how you start a tree for the future.

When a tree gets about a year or two old, it wants to grow like a bush. With a tree that is growing, you cut down the branches that grow on the side and let the center part grow up until the tree gets the height you want. When you have it the height you want, like, for instance, 7 or 8 feet, you cut off the tip of the tree so that the tree will start to branch out on the sides. Don't cut any off the side any more, if you got the height you want. From then on, you let it branch out until it gets the width you want. From then on, you prune regularly every year and cut the branches that touch each other. But don't cut the branches that touch until the fig tree is the height and width that you want.

Don't start pruning the tree until it is at least five years old. If it is a fast-growing tree, you can prune when it gets four years old. We're talking about pruning the inside, but before the tree is five years old, you can cut the suckers that grow on the trunk. Always take them out and let the tree grow up.

Now, how do you prune fig trees? Now, first, when you see a sucker coming from the big trunk, cut it off. We're talking about suckers on the tree, not in the ground. Fig pruning is different than for other fruit trees. If the tree is about 10 or 15 feet high and about 15 feet wide, you stand under the tree and look up. See wherever there are branches that touch together, and cut off the weakest branch so the air can get in All branches that touch each other, you cut the thinnest, skinniest branch off and leave the thicker one. Do this all the way around the tree.

When you've cut off all the branches that touch each other, you go back under the tree and look up again, because sometimes you do miss some.

When you got all that cut off, then stand on the ground and cut off all the branches that have grown down to the ground. Those that you have to bend down to pass through—cut off the branches, until you can stand up. Whatever is lower than your head, cut it off. So next year, when you're going to pick the figs, you don't have to bend down or be careful because you might hit a branch. Also, when the branches are higher than your head, you can see when the figs are ripe or green. And also, the tree looks pretty.

When the trees grow out of form, one side higher than the other, you cut the highest parts level with the other side that is low. All the way around. When you get through pruning, the tree has to look like the shape of an umbrella. And the bottom should be high enough so you can go under and so no one will hit their head on the branches. I'm talking about a tree that is 15 or 20 feet high and 15 or 20 feet wide. Not a tree that is not full grown.

By the way, commercial fig orchards butcher fig trees. They cut them all the way down every year. That's silly, because when you cut the fig trees all the way down, you lose two months.

Their way, first the tree makes shoots and suckers. Then it makes leaves and then it makes figs. By that time, you lose a good two months. Then the figs won't start to get ripe until the first part of August. Before the end of August, they start to get a little cold and in September they drop on the ground before they ripen.

The advantage I get on my figs is that my fig trees make figs before they make leaves. I've had cases when I've picked a few figs by June. From then on, I'll have figs. And I have a good crop. I pick eight, nine, ten boxes on each tree. I have big fig trees with a spread of 25 to 30 feet wide and 25 to 30 feet high. That's how much figs I get out of there. I get ten boxes sometimes. The most you can get the other way is one, one and a half, two boxes from each tree. That's because you cut down up to the trunk. That's a big mistake.

Anybody I ever asked about why they butcher the trees like that, they say, "Well, I get big figs when I do that. If I don't do that, my figs come small." And I tell them that's not so. If you take all the suckers out and you leave a lot of air in the center of the tree, the figs come just as big as when you cut up to the trunk.

With the big trees that you did prune in January, when they start to put out new leaves or throw a lot of suckers, take all the suckers out and when each branch starts to put out six or seven leaves or more, cut off all the old leaves. Be careful not to cut the figs. Leave three or four leaves on the tips of each shoot because they're the ones that the tree breathes through. If you take off all the leaves, the tree will stop breathing and die. Of course, if you haven't got space, and you like a lot of fruit, you have to crowd them, but they won't do so good.

The reason to cut the leaves on the fig trees is so the light of the sun goes through the trees and makes the figs grow big and black, if they are black figs, white, if they are white figs. Not greenish looking. Also, when the sun hits the figs, it brings the flavor into the figs. If you don't cut the leaves, the figs will ripen just the same, but they haven't got no taste. A pale-looking fig is just like a human being that works in the office all the time. They got a pale face because she or he is in the shade all the time. Those particular figs are no good for shipping, especially if you want to send them out of town or out of state. They're too soft because they been growing in the shade.

So you cut the leaves off two times in the season, when they get so thick you can't see through. I do the last cutting of leaves and suckers in April. Stand under the tree and look for the sky. If you can't see the sky, it's time to cut the leaves. If you do that, the figs will get hard and good-tasting. That's the secret to get figs good-looking, good shape and sweet.

People come here and tell me, "How come I bought your fig tree and mine is so small and they haven't got a taste like yours?" Of course, I never did let out my secret, because I been doing it commercially and I don't want anyone to cut the throat on me. But now I release my secret to the public so everybody has a chance. And you can do that with most any kind of fruit trees. You can trim down the leaves or branches so the sun goes through the branches. It doesn't have to be a fig tree.

If you want more than one crop of figs, you have to feed them once a month. If you are in a warm place like here in California, you can have figs until January. That's if you feed and water them. People got the idea that they shouldn't be watered because when you water they make big cracks in the figs. But if from when they start to make leaves you water them once a week and feed them once a month and keep weeding, you can have figs until the end of January. I don't care what anybody says. People tell me the latest you can have figs is October, but I've had good figs until the end of January and as early as June.

On the first of February, you feed the fig trees good because that's when the tree starts to grow and bring the sap up. I would feed them real good food. If you have a lot of chicken manure or rabbit manure or any manure that is kind of strong, they like that. Or blood meal, anything that contains a lot of nitrogen. That's the first feeding.

The second feeding is when the figs get the size of about an inch around. Then you give another good strong feeding so they get a lot of energy to support the figs. Also, they make good-sized fruit and good flavor.

The last feeding is in the first part of August, and you feed them strong. That's if you want figs in November or December. If you want a good commercial crop, you feed every month or month and a half. You get big, good-tasting figs, and the public, as soon as they taste it once, will buy your particular kind of figs all the time. When I take figs to the wholesale market, the storekeeper has two or three hundred boxes of figs, but I've seen people waiting for me to bring figs every Tuesday. And as soon as I bring them, my figs are sold because the people call for them particular kind of figs.

Now we'll talk about how you make your fruit sweet, if your figs don't have much taste. Let's say the tree we were talking about before, 15 or 20 feet high and 15 or 20 feet wide. You make a trench about 3 to 4 feet away from the trunk all the way around, and about 6 to 8 inches deep. Put in the trench no more than two handsful of sea salt. (You can get this at natural foods stores.) Then fill up the trench with water. Or you put one half gallon seawater. First fill up the trench with water and then put the seawater in and be sure you stir up the salt water with the sweet water. If you put the salt alone or the salt water alone, without mixing with the sweet water, eight out of ten you kill the tree.

But if you do like I said, it's just like you do when you put salt in your food. If you put a teaspoon of salt in a pot with three gallons of water and something to cook, it won't taste too salty when you eat it, but if you put a teaspoon of salt in your mouth, it'll burn your mouth. It's the same thing with the tree.

The way I do it, I add salt three times during the season that the tree has fruit. Of course, if that particular fruit is real sweet, you don't have to do that because they get salt from

fertilizer, blood meal and from any kind of soil. But some kind
of trees won't grab all that the soil has. You have to put it
yourself, especially if the tree is an old tree that has been in
the ground for fifteen or twenty years. You have to put in
your own nitrogen and potash because the tree has eaten it all
up after five or six years. You can add salt to any fruit tree.
It doesn't have to be a fig tree.

How you know when the figs are good and ripe? Don't
ever touch a fig even if it looks ripe, because if you squeeze
a fig a little bit it will stop growing and never get ripe. Also,
if you pick figs green, they won't get ripe because they keep
feeding from the mother until they are ripe. So how can you
tell if they are ripe or not?

When the figs start to droop on the branches, look on the
bottom of the fig. There will be a hole. If it is .pen and you
can see inside, then the fig is ready to pick. If the hole is still
closed and tight, don't pick the fig because it's not ripe and
will have no taste. That's the way the stores buy them, because they have to keep two or three days in the store. The
store doesn't care what the merchandise tastes like; they just
don't want any to get rotten. But you wait another two or
three days until the hole is open. This is important. If you're
growing to sell commercially, pick the figs when the holes start
to open up. (We're talking about any figs except Mission figs;
they never crack and make holes.)

Sometimes the figs crack too much. The crack splits open
and you can't sell them, but it's good to eat. But they won't
ripen right. When they crack fast like that, that means that
you kept them dry for a while and then watered all at once.
The plant grabs the water fast and the fruit cracks because it
grows too fast. But if you've been watering the tree at least
once a week, they never will crack. If you didn't water the
tree for two, three or four weeks, don't water it all at once.
Just give little tiny bits of water each day. They will still

crack, but not right open so you can't use them. That's for most all figs.

If you want to dry figs, you can use strawberry or Kadota figs. You have to wait until the figs are just about to fall from the tree. Otherwise, you can't dry them. When the fig is dead ripe, drooping on the branch, that's the fig you can pick to dry. You put them in the sun. You dry them very dry and store them. I usually store them in a plastic bag so they keep good. But don't leave them in the open. If you do, the moths go to the figs, lay eggs on them and eat them and you can't eat them. Moths do like figs. But when you put them in a plastic bag and seal them, no moths will get in there.

Strawberry figs and Kadota figs are the only ones I dry. Of course, Mission can be dried too, but they have to have a real hot climate like Las Vegas or Palm Springs. But around here in Malibu or Los Angeles, the weather is not hot enough. If you do want to dry them here, put them in the sun in the daytime, and in the nighttime bring them in. Don't leave them out because the dew will fall on the figs and they get moldy. But if you take them daytime out, nighttime in, they dry perfect.

That's the story of figs, or most fruit trees. Now remember this: don't ever leave any suckers on the trees because they take all the energy the tree has and keep it from the fruit. Usually the suckers get big and husky. That goes for any kind of trees. That's all we have on figs.

12

MUSHROOMS

I've been having a lot of requests on how you raise mushrooms.

First you have to make a special compost. You get a bale of hay, you buy the cheapest you can get, or you go where they have a lot of dry weeds and you cut them off and gather them until you have about a bale of weeds about 5 feet long, 4 feet wide and 4 feet high. You get a bucket or a big pan and fill it with water and you dip the hay in the water. It has to be well soaked. Then you put the hay in a pile, and you soak the hay two times a day with a hose for two days. In the morning and in the night.

On the third day that the hay has been soaking, it is time to make a compost pile. I do it with my hands because I don't do much. If you plan to do a lot, you get a pitchfork. Make a clean and level spot about three feet from where you got the pile. You make a layer of hay the same size as the first pile, 5 feet by 4 feet, and about 3 inches thickness. Don't make the layers too thick. Then sprinkle some chicken manure or rabbit manure, and a little blood meal. You repeat these layers until you use all of the pile of hay that you have been wetting. I want to mention too that if you want better service you can put a layer of alfalfa hay about 1 to 2 inches thick on top of the layers of blood meal. And you have a little quicker service to make the mushrooms.

Now, you leave the pile for three days. In three days you turn it over and make another pile. Take a little bit of hay at a time, and when you take it off you go from one end and turn it over onto the other pile. Be sure that all the outside hay and the top hay goes in the center of the new pile, and the center hay has to go on the outside. It has to be well turned over and not in clumps. You have to do a little bit at a time. You start from the top and go straight down and you make a similar pile. Eventually, you will turn the pile at least three times.

The idea is that inside the pile it gets real hot. And the outside is cold. If you have any kind of thermometer that goes up to 150 degrees F, then you put that thermometer in the pile. You can make an extension for your thermometer by using a piece of copper tubing. The copper is a very good conductor. It should get about 150 degrees F. Even 125 to 140 degrees is good. It has to be over 125 degrees F, and if you mix your layers right it will get 125 degrees on the second day that you have that pile. If the pile doesn't get hot enough, wait an extra day or two before you turn it over.

Now, if it reaches 125 degrees on the first day, in the first eight hours, or 150 degrees before the third day, you have too much fertilizer in the pile, too much chicken or rabbit manure. You won't have too much blood meal, because blood meal isn't hot enough. What you do is you add more hay or you wash it off a little bit. By washing it off you won't know how much nitrogen you wash off. So I would add more hay. Of course you have to wait another day extra.

If the mixture is done right, the second time you turn the pile over you will see some white streak mold in the center.

After the third turn, you don't turn the hay any more. Then you let it sit another three or four days. That's at least twelve days in all. There should be lots of stringy mold. After it sits the three or four days, this hay, what we call compost now, has to be sterilized in an oven with a heat of 250 to 300 degrees. If you can't do that, then it needs to be sterilized with burning sulfur.

To sterilize with burning sulfur, you get a box, turn it upside down, and you put all the compost on top of the box. You leave a hole in the box big enough to stick your hands in. You put the compost on top and you put a sulfur candle inside.

If you can't get a sulfur candle, you can make one. Take a can about 3 inches high and about 1 inch in diameter. Or use the inside from a toilet paper roll. You can make a wick by taking string from a potato sack or any kind of burlap sack. You keep winding strings around until you have made it ⅛ inch thick. Put the wick in the center of the can with some sulfur mixed with a little gasoline, and let the mixture dry before you use it.

You put all the hay compost on the top, light the sulfur candle underneath and then you cover it up pretty good with cloth or a piece of plastic or whatever you have, even paper, if you got enough cheap paper. But be sure the fumes from the sulfur stay inside. Make sure the candle is burning well before you cover it up. And you let it stay that way all night and all day.

Stay away from the fumes. They won't kill you but they will choke you. The fumes from the sulfur are not poison, because if they were I would be dead fifty years ago. The fumes from the sulfur are gone five minutes after you uncover the compost. You will have no trouble at all with the mushrooms or to breathe yourself.

Then get the compost and put it in a good-sized box. Try not to disturb the compost or stir it up any more. Apple boxes are a good size, or you can make a box 12 inches deep, 24 inches long and 12 inches wide, something like that. The thickness of the compost, when you make mushrooms, should never be any less than 8 inches when you put it in the box. Every 3 inches of compost you sprinkle mushroom seed, until you fill up the box.

Now, where you get the mushroom seed is a problem. You can get the mushroom seed by finding out who grows them and buy from him or if you have a problem and you are in Los Angeles or near where I am, 30040 Morning View Drive, Malibu, write to me or come over. If I have some handy I will give it to you or sell it to you or tell you where to get it.

The mushroom seed is made with spores from mushroom. The laboratories mix wheat or white millet or yellow millet with the spores to make it easier to seed the compost. If you seed with mushroom spores alone, they are too fine and you would put too much in one place and not enough in another place. But if you mix the spores with the millet or wheat you can put it even.

You spread the mushroom seed on top of the compost, and keep making layers of compost and seed until you fill the flat up to 2 inches from the top. Don't put any compost on the last layer of seed. You water the compost once and forget about it until mold starts to come on top. After one and a half or two weeks it should be solid mold. Then you put from 1 to 1½ inches of soil on top of that. The soil mixture should be one part red clay and one part heavy, sandy soil, mixed well. If you want to be safe and have no trouble, you put

40 percent peat moss in the soil mixture. I recommend German peat moss, but if you haven't got German peat moss, any kind will do. Then you put this mixture on top of the compost in the boxes, but don't pack it. After you put the soil in, you water it once and that's it.

Then you cover it up with a wet burlap sack. The sacks are kept damp, maybe wetting them every morning or every evening, but don't water the compost or soil any more.

Make sure the soil and peat moss mixture stays damp. When you see the mold coming up through the soil you raise up the sacks about four or five inches high and keep wetting them every day. Don't let the sacks touch your soil mixture because the mushrooms will become spotty. They still will be good eating, but they don't look good. Raise up with sticks or anything you have, but still they have to be covered. Wet the sacks only, not the compost. Take the sacks off, soak them in a bucket, and put them back on top.

In ten to fifteen days you will have mushrooms. Don't ever cut the mushrooms you have in the box. You pull them out by hand and make sure you pull all the roots out. If you don't, you will never have any more mushrooms in that box because the roots rot. So pull all mushrooms out with the roots, soil and all. After each crop, you water the soil, but that's the only time you water anything but the sacks.

After I have picked three crops of mushrooms, I put a little more soil in the boxes to replace the soil that comes out when you pick the mushrooms. I would water the new soil outside the boxes, in a bucket or can or whatever you have it in, and then sprinkle it on top. And still every day I keep the sacks on top of the boxes wet.

Every eight days, for eighty days or more, you will have mushrooms. So all the work you do at the beginning is not a waste, because you get so many mushrooms out of there it isn't funny. If you try to buy mushrooms at 95 cents a pound, they run a lot of money. And you don't know if they are organic, even if they tell you that they are organic. But when you do it yourself you know they are organic.

This is very important. The mushrooms need lots of ventilation, fresh air. It is not necessary that they be grown in a dark spot. All you need is a lot of ventilation and damp humidity in the air. By having ventilation and humidity in the air, you have good mushrooms. The way you make humidity in the air is by putting the wet sacks on top of the boxes. A good way to get good ventilation is to use a cellar, because a cellar has a lot of vents all around the building and they give a lot of fresh air. Of course, you can put a fan near by the mushrooms to make ventilation, but the best places are a patio, a garage (keep the doors open) or use an abandoned car you have sitting around. Just don't let it get too hot.

Mushrooms can stand temperatures up to 65 degrees F, but over 65 degrees your mushrooms become very skinny, the heads are very flat, and they have no taste. You may have to control the heat with a fan. They can't stand it lower than 50 degrees, or higher than 65 degrees. Fifty-five to sixty is perfect.

How you pick mushrooms. Some people, they like little button size, 1 to 1½ inch. I don't like them that way. No taste. I let the mushrooms grow till they open from the bottom and get 3 to 4 inches. I like them better that way. But the growers, they think it is no good when they are that big. In fact, no one will buy one when it is like that because, as with anything, they have to look nice and perfect. People see a big mushroom and they won't buy, but that's when they got good taste and good flavor.

In Chapter 16 I tell the way I cook mushrooms. You see what you taste. It's out of this world. Then you never buy any more little mushrooms; you ask for the biggest you can get.

Usually, though, the big ones are very hard to find, unless

you know a place like mine or you go to the mushroom grower. Sometimes they have some big ones because they have missed a day of picking. If they do have any they will be glad to sell them to you because the stores don't like them, but believe me they are the best. And that's my experience. This is Frank Bucaro. Everybody know me by Chico.

13

GRAPES

We are about at the end of November and we are going to talk about how we prune grapes and how you will know if the vines are going to make grapes the next year or not. This is for this part of the country, in California. If it is any other part of the country, you start to prune grapes when all the moisture is out of the leaves, because if you prune them before that, they'll start to sprout and they won't make much grapes the following spring.

When you prune grapes, if it is your first pruning after planting them the year before, you cut off the first one or two or three eyes from where the soil starts and leave the next three above that. Then prune above that. What we call eyes is where the leaves grow.

The idea of cutting the first three eyes is that when they start to sprout and make grapes, the grapes won't touch the ground. Because when the grapes or flowers touch the ground, they'll start to mold and they'll fall down. You can do another

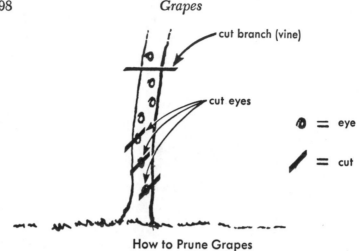

cut branch (vine)

cut eyes

🍷 = eye

／ = cut

How to Prune Grapes

thing. You can stick them. When they get about a foot or a foot and a half high, you tie them up to a stake.

How will you know if the plants will make grapes or not? That's a little trick that most pruners don't know. When you prune, leave three or four eyes on the branches that made grapes the year before. If the branch made grapes the year before, you can depend that it will make grapes the following year. That's number one. Number two: on the branches that didn't make grapes the year before, cut the branch all the way to the stem.

Also, you keep the strongest eye there is. If the eye is pretty thick and fat, it'll be a strong eye even if the branch didn't have grapes the year before. Maybe it won't make grapes this particular year either. Leave it anyway.

To plant new grape vines, you always get the cuttings from the branches that come up from the old vine. Always take them from a vine that had grapes. Don't plant the tip of a branch, because if you do you'll lose three years. They won't make grapes the same year or the second year. Another thing I would recommend, when you make a cutting to plant in the ground, make a real sharp cut, because if it isn't sharp the branch will bruise and start to decay and mold. I usually leave from six to eight eyes on the branch. I put three eyes in the ground and water it and pack it. And four eyes I leave on top of the ground. Then, I'll cut the two bottom eyes and leave the two top eyes. It is important to cut the two eyes above the ground right after you plant them. Cut them close enough so they won't grow. So all the strength from the stem goes to the two or three eyes you left on.

When the new shoot starts to get a foot and a half or two feet, if it has grapes or not, dust it with dusting sulfur because grapes have a tendency to make black fungus. They live the first year, but the fungus gets in the wood, and the next year, it'll probably shoot one or two little shoots and it'll be very weak. In two or three years that plant will die.

If the plant makes grapes, you dust the grapes and the stem. You got to dust them three times in the season, about a month apart. The reason is, so the grapes will have full bunches. You won't lose any grapes out of the bunch. It makes a nice, tight bunch. Otherwise, you'll get one or two or three bad grapes that will spread to the branch. But you save your branch by dusting and you save the grapes.

After a branch with grapes gets 6 to 8 inches away from the grapes or flowers, pinch that particular branch so the strength from the stem goes to the grapes instead of to the tip. If the stem doesn't make grapes, don't pinch it, because that stem will make grapes the following year.

Sometimes when you plant cuttings, not all the plants you put in the ground will live. Sometimes you get 70 or 80 percent. If you're lucky, you'll get 90. But there is another way you can replace the plants that die. With the branch that you leave alone, if you got a space near the plant, the following year bend the longest branches down and put them under the ground and let them come up about 3 feet away from the

mother one and pack the ground hard. Put it a foot or a foot
and a half deep and let it come up on the other end. Then
you'll leave them alone until the second year. That's when I
usually give them another dusting of sulfur.

You have to feed the grapes. The first good feed you give is
right after you prune them. You feed something strong like
chicken manure or rabbit manure. Some people use bat
manure. Anything high in nitrogen. Then you feed them again
when they're the size of marbles. When they get that size,
you give them a good feed and a good water. From then on,
if the place is dry with no humidity, you have to water every
week. If there is a lot of humidity or a lot of rain, you don't
have to water. In Italy, we never water grapes, and we have
a lot of good grapes and a lot of good wine.

About in August, the grapes start to show little light spots.
That means they are starting to get ripe. Don't do nothing
after that except water them. Water steady and regular if it
is dry country.

If you are commercial and you are going to sell the grapes
to stores, don't let the grapes get dead ripe because if you do,
by the time you take them to the market and sell to the
stores and the stores sell to the public, the grapes will be
pretty rotten and a man that bought your grapes will never
buy from you any more.

If you are going to use the grapes for your table, don't pick
them all at once because grapes don't ripen all at once. You
pick the grapes that are nice and yellow whenever you need
them and you put them in a bowl on the table and they
stay two, three, four days.

If you're going to use the grapes to make raisins and you've
got a lot of birds, put a scarecrow or a record that makes a
sound like a shot every two or three minutes and the birds
will be scared and go away.

To make raisins, you pick the grapes when they get brownish and kind of mushy like (in California, from November first to tenth or fifteenth). You cut the grapes, but don't take them off the branches. You put a string on each bunch of grapes and hang them where there is a lot of air, a lot of ventilation. When there is no more moisture, I take the raisins off and package them in a cardboard carton. Never use any tin or metal to store figs, grapes or anything dry.

When you put them in the cardboard box, you can store them any place you want. Of course you have to be careful that moths don't get in there. If you want to keep grapes a long time you have to put them in a cool place. Find the coolest place there is, because moths do like grapes and then you'll get bugs in there and they won't be fit to eat. So that's the situation with grapes.

What we have been talking about is for muscatel grapes, because that's what I like most. Never try to make raisins from any kind of black grapes because they won't do it. Of course, they might, but I myself haven't been able to make raisins out of black grapes of any kind. You can make raisins out of seedless grapes. Also, seedless grapes are early grapes, and you don't have to wait like you do with muscatel grapes. Both seedless and Concord are early grapes. You can make good wine out of black grapes.

To make wine out of grapes (this is for California) don't ever use grapes until they are dead ripe. If they're not, there are two things you can have out of that: vinegar or grapes that become bitter and have no taste. And the chances are that they will spoil before you get wine.

When they're good and ripe, there is no sour taste at all, and you make good wine. Now, don't you ever think that you have to take the grapes out of the bunch to make wine, because you can squash the stems with the grapes and they will bring better flavor. And if you know that they are organic grapes, if they're your own, not bought, don't wash them because when you wash grapes you take all the good out of them. Of course if they're not organic, you wash them. But you can only wash what is on top. What's inside the grapes, you can't wash. What's in there is in there. You can't take it off. But still you can make good wine even if you do wash them, as long as they're ripe and sweet. Remember, them grapes have got to be sweet. Even if the grapes are dead ripe, if they're not sweet, they won't make good wine.

14

WINEMAKING

I've had requests to teach how to make a good wine. The people that make good wine, few of them are left. Here's how to make wine.

First, prepare your barrel. I never recommend to put wine in a jar or glass. You get a wood barrel. Remember this: not a barrel that has ever had vinegar in it, because the wine you make will turn to vinegar. You get a barrel that has had whiskey, alcohol, wine. That's a good barrel. Make two holes in the barrel. One about 2 inches across, on what we call the belly, and another smaller hole in the bottom of the barrel.

Then you have to sterilize your barrel. First, you wash it good. Then, you get a gunnysack and make a long piece like a string out of it, ¼ inch around. Wet the string and dip it in sulfur. (Sometimes you can buy sulfur strings.) After it dries, light the string and put it inside the hole. You open both holes. After the string with sulfur burns down, the barrel is well sterilized and you can cork both holes until you put in

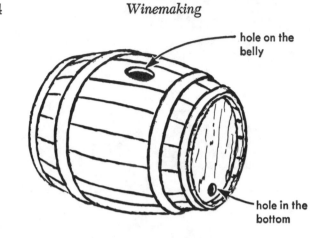

hole on the
belly

hole in the
bottom

Wine Barrel

the grape juice. I would recommend using round pieces of
wood instead of corks.

The secret of making good strong wine is the barrel. You
get two pounds carob pods, two pounds dried figs, two pounds

carob
mixture

Soaking the Barrel

raisins, one or two gallons of grape juice that you've made from fresh grapes. Put them in a pot and let it boil. After they been boiling about an hour or an hour and a half, you get the mixture from the grapes, raisins, figs and carob, turn the barrel straight up and fill up the ring on top of the barrel with the mixture. Let it stay on there twenty-four hours so that it soaks into the wood. Then you turn the barrel upside down and fill up the other side with the mixture. And let it stay twenty-four hours. After that, whatever juice you got left, put inside the barrel and plug up the small hole. Then you roll the barrel around so the juice gets all over. For the inside, use just the juice, not the whole mixture.

Now, how to make wine. You get grapes that are well ripe. They have to be ripe. You squash the grapes, grind them and make a juice out of them. Then you press them and use the carob, raisins and figs that you got left, and grind them together with the grapes. When you have made the juice, put it in the barrel, which should be lying on its side, and leave the big hole open. Let it ferment slowly for eight to ten to fifteen days in a cool place like a cellar, if you have one, or inside a garage. How do you know when the wine stops fermenting? You light a match and put it on top of the hole. If the flame goes up, or the match goes out, it's still fermenting. If the flame doesn't move, that means it's stopped fermenting. I wait three more days and then cork the barrel very tight with a piece of wood.

I can't tell you exactly how many days it should ferment because it all depends on the weather. If the days are colder, it takes longer. If it is warm, it takes less. You have to use your own judgment.

Let it stand for four to six months. After six months, drill a little hole. Let some of the wine come out and taste it to see if it is good. If it is no good, cork it again with another little piece of wood and wait a little longer.

Wherever you're going to store the wine, make a little bench and put the barrels lengthwise on top of the bench with the big cork on top. Before you put them on the bench, you stand them up with the small cork on top and put on a spigot if you want. You put a regular wooden spigot and close it good. Then you put them on top of the bench with the spigot down.

Never open the top cork, the one on the belly. That's real important. Even if the wine comes very slowly out of the small spigot, on the bottom, don't try to open the top cork, because if you do open the top cork, you'll let air in the barrel. And when you have air in the barrel, the wine turns sour. It makes vinegar. But when you take from the bottom spigot all the time, it draws all the air from the barrel and that wine, from the top to the bottom, up to the last drop, will be perfect like the first time you take it out. That's real important. That's the trick and the secret of the wine in the barrel.

A lot of people have trouble and come to me and say, "Why does my wine turn sour?" And I tell them exactly what I been saying now. They say, "Well, I haven't got a barrel. I put it in a jar or a five-gallon can and every time I want wine, I tip it over." Now that's the biggest mistake. They sell little barrels from one gallon on up, if you don't want to make too much wine. And still they have two holes; one on the bottom and another one on the belly. The idea is to get every drop of wine without opening the top hole on the belly.

Now, let's go back to when you squeeze the grapes. After you finish squeezing, you grind the pulp again and put it back in the presser and squeeze it again. You'll get more juice. After you get all the juice out of the grapes the second time, put the pulp in an open barrel and put some water in there. Let it sit overnight or twenty-four hours. Then put it in the presser and squeeze it again. And you get more juice. But don't mix this up with the other juice, because this is the wine that you buy for $1.75 or $2.00 a gallon. This is the

large hole
with wood cork

small hole
for spigot

Storing the Barrels

cheap wine, after you put in water and let it set. You can do this another time the same way.

After the second time that you make the cheap wine, you get the same pulp that has been with water two times and put it in a barrel. Let's say a barrel with fifteen gallons of water. For fifteen gallons of water, put in ten pounds of sugar. And about five cakes of yeast. Let it ferment again for another eight or ten days. Then you squeeze it and cook it. You make brandy.

Now, if you want to know how you make brandy or alcohol, you get a regular hot-water kettle. See if you can get a hot water kettle made of stainless steel, or even you can get brass or copper, but not aluminum. Then you go to any plumber and get a plumber's pipe tee, a ¾-inch stainless steel or brass plug and three or four feet of ¼-inch stainless steel tubing. The tee has to have an opening of ¾-inch diameter on one side, and the other side should be the same size as the tubing. You take off the little cap on the kettle that whistles when the water boils and you put the tee where the cap was and take it to any place that can weld the tee on the kettle. Put one hole straight up and one hole straight out of the tee. When it is welded, you make a coil out of the piece of tubing, connect one end to the tee and bend the tubing some way to get the other end inside a bucket with water.

When you have all these parts connected, you put the juice in the kettle and put it on the stove and let it cook. When it starts to boil, what comes out of the tubing is brandy. Be sure the tubing is more than half inside the bucket with the water. Put a hose with cold water running inside the bucket. The colder the water is, the more alcohol or brandy you get out of the tubing.

Now, this is very important: see that the liquid in the kettle never runs out. Before it does, you put in more juice. The idea of putting the tee on the kettle is that you have one hole

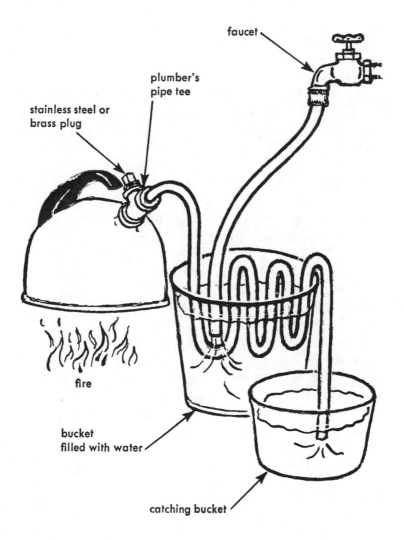

faucet

plumber's
pipe tee

stainless steel or
brass plug

fire

bucket
filled with water

catching bucket

Device for Making Brandy or Alcohol

on the top where you put the liquid, and another hole for
the brandy to come out of. After you finish putting liquid, you
put the stainless steel or brass plug. They never get rusty and
harmful. An iron plug will get rusty, and that's no good for
your body.

If you want to make alcohol out of that, about 150 or 175
proof, after you cook it the first time, recook it. The first time,
you only get 60 or 75 proof. Sometimes you get 80 proof. It
makes good brandy, but for alcohol you have to cook it again
to make it stronger. With alcohol, you can preserve things. I
make hair tonic that I keep from fermenting and spoiling by
putting 5 to 10 percent alcohol. It will keep forever. Anything
liquid that you want to keep, there are three things you can
put in there: alcohol, sugar or salt. When you do that, you can
keep it for five to ten years without any trouble at all.

Now we go back to the brandy and the kettle. On the other
end, where the steam comes out, you put a bottle so you catch
it. Whatever comes boiling out of the tubing is brandy or
alcohol.

If you want to make sweet wine out of the wine you made
before, don't ever put in sugar. You get ten gallons of the
juice you've been squeezing and put with it one gallon of
the alcohol that you've been making. Before the wine starts
to ferment. You got to put the alcohol in the grape juice
before it ferments. Otherwise you won't have sweet wine.
You still will have dry wine. Of course, it will be strong. But
if you put alcohol when you finish making the grape juice,
then you plug it and put it away.

In five or six months, you'll have Marsala. Instead of letting
it age twenty-five or thirty years, you'll have Marsala in
four or five months. And it's the same Marsala. What is
Marsala? Marsala is wine that we used to give to TB—
tuberculosis—people to build up their body. Because tuberculosis people are very skinny and they haven't got energy.

A little glass, two-ounce glass, of Marsala wine, two ounces in the morning, two ounces in the noon and two ounces at nighttime, will build up their body and make it strong, and we have a chance to cure the tuberculosis.

Of course, they have to be in the country where the fresh air is. Not in the city, because in the city they have a lot of germs. But in the country where there are a lot of trees, the trees absorb the bad germs and purify the air. And with a chance like that, anyone who has TB, by eating good, you will cure the TB.

That's the end of making wine. This is Frank Bucaro, and everybody know me by Chico.

15

BEES

First let's talk about the box to put the bees in. If you
don't know anything about raising bees, I suggest that you
buy the box ready-made. You can buy the boxes from bee-
keepers or from mail-order catalogs. Make sure each box you
buy has a comb with wax already in it. The whole thing
should cost about $12.00 a box.

When you get your boxes, set each one out of the wind
under a tree. Next you have to get bees. One way is to order
them too, from a beekeeper or honey store or mail-order
catalog. You have to order at least a month or two in advance.
But I never get my bees this way.

I get my bees when I see a swarm in the woods or in a
private yard. I ask the owner and they're glad for me to take
them. Or sometimes I put an ad in the paper and they call
me to get them from their yard. If the bees are high in a tree,
I charge the owner to take them out of there. If it is easy, I
get them and the owner is glad to have them gone, because

he's scared. A lot of people, when they have bees on their property, call the sheriff's department. So if you register with the sheriff, they will call you when someone calls them.

How do you pick them from where they are? When you see bees on a branch, all together, take the box you bought from the beekeeper and take a clipper. Before you put the box under the branch, you put some honey or sugar that has been dissolved in water (make it pretty thick) in the box. You put the box under the clump of bees that is in the tree and you cut the branch very slowly without disturbing the bees. Hold the branch while you cut it so it doesn't fall. You let it drop down slowly on top of the box with the comb in it and the honey inside the comb or box. Very slowly.

Usually the queen is right in the center of the clump. If they're in a swarm, they don't have a home and there's nothing to eat until they find a place: a hole inside a tree, a hole inside a wall, inside a roof. So if you put some honey in your bee box, they will be glad to make themselves at home there.

How do you take care of bees after you have them? I would advise to put the bee box on top of another plain box with the slope toward the front. That is in case it rains, the water won't get in the front.

Watch out for ants getting in the bee box, because ants like honey. The best way to control ants is to put legs on the hive box and put the legs in water. You get a couple plastic bottles and cut them in half straight across. The idea to use plastic is so they won't rust. You cut the bottles in half and you put each leg inside a plastic bottle and you fill it up full of water. The bottle has to be at least 5 inches because the ants make bridges by each other. They run one after the other on top of each other and they go inside to get the food. I've seen that done.

The bee has another enemy. That's moths. The moth gets in and lays eggs like a queen and walks like a queen and sometimes the bees get confused. The moth hides herself for two or three times and then goes out in the open. And she lays eggs in the corner and she lays eggs right inside the comb and pretty soon the moths start hatching, and if there are too many moths, the bees leave. That's the biggest problem I ever find.

The way you control that: every week you open the box, you lift it up slowly and look for the moths. At the same time you look for the queen bee, because then you start to get familiar with the bees and the bees start to get familiar with you and you recognize the queen and you recognize the drones. Usually when I see a drone, I take it away from there because the drone won't go to work. Drones just eat the honey. You can tell a drone because it has the biggest head and eyes, and drones have flat bodies, whereas workers have pointed bodies. A drone is smaller than a queen, but bigger than a worker. The drones are males and the workers are females.

You have to be very careful every time you open the box to look at the comb, because sometimes you get a horny worker bee and they make a comb full of drone cells. You see, the queen can make any kind of egg she wants. Worker egg, drone egg, queen egg, depending on the size of the hole the workers make. If the queen lays drones on the cells, you have a comb full of drones. And you know how many holes are in the comb? From 700 to 900 holes. And that's a small comb. That many drones will be born inside the hive. And when you see that, you take it off, because if you have that many drones in the box they eat all the honey. A drone never goes to work.

The bees have crews. One crew to clean up the house, one crew to go out and get the pollen and sugar out of the flowers and bring it in. Another crew makes the little houses, the holes where the honey is and where the bees are born. Another crew straightens the holes. When the holes are made, the queen makes eggs, one after the other all day long. Another crew seals the holes after they are full of honey.

The bees have guards that stand right in front of the hive, and when a worker bee comes in, they see that she drops the honey and goes out again. If the worker bee can't go to work any more or doesn't want to work any more, they'll kill her. Or if there is a few drones in there, they'll kill them. All the bees in there have to do something, or it's no good for them. They'll kill them. That's the workers. But when there are too many drones, they can't kill them all, and they can't kill ants because they're too small for the stinger.

It takes about nineteen days to get bees after the queen starts to lay eggs in the holes in the comb. Before they hatch, you need another box called a super that is used for storing surplus honey. It fits on top of your first box. In this super, ten combs will fit, but never put in more than nine. In some boxes, you put in eight combs, but if you don't put in at least one comb less than will fit, you won't be able to pull them out when they have honey in them. It will stick.

You take the top off the first box and put the super on top. The super hasn't got any bottom. Wherever you buy the super, you have to get the screen that goes under. Don't make it yourself. The screen is so the queen can't go over to the super and start laying eggs. If she does that you won't have no honey. The super is all for the workers. The holes in the screen are made just big enough for the workers. Not for the queen. That way you get the honey after the honey is sealed. When the holes are full, the bees seal them, and that's the time to get the honey out of there. If you get it before that, the honey is not perfect and it gets sour. Sometimes it gets too thin and isn't much good to eat.

The bees have a crew inside the hive that fans when it is too hot. They dry the honey and make it thick. Their job is just to fan all the time. When the workers bring the sugar

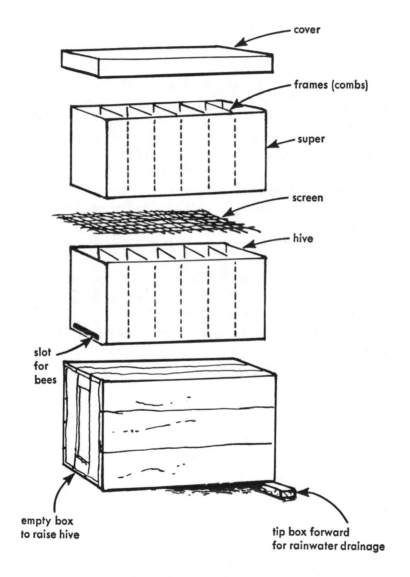

cover

frames (combs)

super

screen

hive

slot
for
bees

empty box
to raise hive

tip box forward
for rainwater drainage

Bee Hive, Super and Box

from the flowers, it's very liquid, like water. They put it in and the crew starts to fan right away. And when the hole is full, they have a crew we call the capping. They put on the capping. Then it's ready to pick.

Sometimes I didn't put anything on me when I used to get the honey, but you get yourself a smoker or a mask and gloves and a suit. Lift up the cover from the top, the super. And lift up the combs one by one and replace with clean ones. Ask at the place where you buy the box and wax, and he'll tell you what you need. Now this is very important. A secret I've never let out. If you want honey often and a lot of honey, I'll tell you what to do.

Lift up the super, and very carefully put it on top of another box. After you take your honey, before you put the clean combs in, you look down below in the box where the queen is and look at every comb. If you have combs inside with a lot of bees, before they hatch you put them on top in the super (be sure you don't put the queen on top). You brush all the adult bees down below so you don't make a mistake. Put just little baby bees, before they're born, inside the super. Put three or four combs in between the empty combs. Put some in the center, some on the side.

What happens is, when they are born, they won't know any place else but the super. A bee, as soon as it is born, goes out to work. They go to work, and when they come back they go through the queen hive and to the super because that's the only place they know because they were born in there. If you don't do that, the bees in the super will die or be missing and get fewer and fewer all the time.

If you don't put the bees in the super before they're born, they won't go on top of there because they won't know how to get there. But if you put the babies before they're born, you have fast honey.

Another thing I want to remind you, don't ever put a comb

that had drones in with the queen because the queen will lay
more drone eggs in it. You put combs for workers only in the
queen's box. If you have holes for drones, put that comb on
top in the super.

The hole for the drones is a little bigger than the hole for
the worker. If you look carefully at the holes, you'll see that
the drone is always a little bigger. The hole for the queen
is made like a hook and usually is on the edge of the frame,
on the bottom. Sometimes it is on the side. And usually you
find drones right around the queen. Sometimes right on the
edge, all the way around the frame. When I see that in the
queen's box, I break the drone holes and let it start all over
again. If you haven't got so many horny bees in there, they'll
rebuild for the worker. But if they rebuild for the drones
again, break them down again. That's the best secret to get
a lot of honey out of the box. I used to get 50 to 60 pounds
per super every month. A lot of bee men never would believe
that, but I got so much because I raise flowers that the bees
like.

I raise these flowers so the workers won't get out of my
property. My property never was without flowers. And I have
true organic honey. I've seen bees travel two miles to get
food, and when they go out away from your farm, the place
where you are, how do you know the other places in the
neighborhood don't spray? I won't take the chance. I plant
flowers all over that bees like. They like statice and finochio.
They like basil. They go crazy for basil. They like anise. They
like marrubium. They like sage. They go crazy for eucalyptus.
They like oranges, lemon, grapefruit. When they haven't got
that, they go out and get any wild flower.

I've never seen bees, in my experience, go to flowers that
are poisonous, and I've raised poisonous plants just to see if
the bees would go to them. They don't. One more thing: in

the winter you have to keep the bees warm and feed them water with honey or sugar.

How to keep honey. You get the honey out of the hive, you cut it in pieces from the comb, and you put it in a collander. Let it drain overnight. You can eat the wax and the capping. It's good to eat and good for you. But if you don't like that, get honey that's been drained. Don't ever put honey in a cold place, in the icebox. Put it in a warm place, on top of the stove. Don't ever heat up the honey directly on a fire if it gets thick because it will lose everything in it.

If the honey does get thick, you can put it in a double boiler and let it warm up very slowly, not fast or high, until it gets to liquid. That way it won't get sour. If you let it boil, it won't taste good. That's my experience.

16

HOW TO COOK
THE ITALIAN WAY

How you make your own spice for cooking, like for soup, for roast, for Italian sauce? You get celery seed, parsley seed, raw black peppers, a little bit cayenne peppers. Adaghiro. If you haven't got adaghiro, substitute bay leaves. You get rose hips, the same rose hips that you make a tea out of, and the seed from the regular roses and leaves (petals) from roses. Also add *basilico* (sweet basil) and cloves and a stick of cinnamon which you make into small crumb pieces. You dry all these things together and store them away until it's completely dry. If you want to do it better yet, after you have all this mixture, you put it in a blender and grind it.

If you make a roast, or roast chicken, you put the roast in the oven, put some butter on top of the roast and sprinkle a little bit of the seasoning that you grinded and let them cook together. You never taste anything like it.

If you make soup and you want to make real good chicken soup—or broth, or vegetable soup—when you put the chicken in the pot with the water, you put a half teaspoon of the ground spice for each gallon of water. You'll get a taste that's out of this world. Of course you put salt and pepper like you want them. I would put some tomatoes or, if you haven't got any, put some tomato sauce. And anybody who drinks that soup will lick his fingers.

If you want to make real honest-to-goodness Italian sauce, you take tomatoes that are absolutely ripe on the vine. If you raise them yourself, let them get dead ripe in the field and then you pick them. I do recommend Italian tomatoes or what are called plum tomatoes. Not the yellow one, the red one. Because plum tomatoes got more meat and not much water. For twenty quarts, you get ten pounds of real ripe figs and thirty pounds of tomatoes. You wash both, clean them, cut them in pieces, put them in a pot and boil. With this thirty pounds of tomatoes you put three pounds onions. You peel them, chop them and put them with the tomatoes and the figs. Also put in about four ounces green *basilico* (sweet basil), four ounces bay leaves, two good hot peppers and enough salt for your taste, and cook them all together.

Let it all cook not any less than three hours from when they start to boil. After they been boiling three hours, you grind them like with regular tomato sauce. I usually get my blender and grind everything, skin and all, except I take out the bay leaves. Then I peel a clove of garlic and chop it into very small pieces and fry it with one cup olive oil. When the garlic starts to get brown in the frying pan, not before, then you throw it in with the tomatoes, figs, onion, basil, bay leaves and peppers and stir it up. Also add three quarters of a tablespoon of your ground spice.

Then put it all on top of the fire again and cook for another half hour. Then you put it in jars and seal them. If you want to keep the sauce for a long time, be very generous with the salt and black peppers. Otherwise the sauce will get sour overnight. Try to put the sauce in the jar the same day that you make it. Close the jars tight and boil the jars for 30 minutes. The water in the pot should cover the jars. Let the jars cool upside down to see if they leak. If a jar leaks, tighten it and boil it again. This is more important than making the sauce itself. Be sure the figs are real ripe. What the figs do to the sauce is they take all the acid off the tomatoes. I've had cases of some people who couldn't eat tomato sauce or tomatoes because they got a lot of acid. But the figs cut down all the acid and you can eat them without any trouble. That's for spaghetti sauce or anything else, like roast or salad or soup.

Now, if you do like Italian sausage, and some people are crazy for it, you don't have to go out and buy Italian sausage for $1.50 or $1.75 a pound. I seen some places for $2.00 a pound. You can make your own very simply. There's nothing to it.

You get one or two pounds hamburger, depending on how many people you have to feed. If you have two pounds of hamburger, you put a good pinch of fennel seed, or you can make your own fennel seed. Around here in California wild fennel grows all over. Of course, domestic fennel would be better, but if you haven't got that, get wild fennel and keep the seed for whenever you make sausage. You put the fennel in the hamburger. You put salt and pepper. I would put heavy on the grinded or raw black pepper. Not the way you usually eat pepper on food. Make it a little heavy.

To make a good sausage you have to have a piece of pork or pork meat, or get a piece of lard, chop it down and mix it with the hamburger. About a quarter pound of pork lard will do. That's a cheap way to do it and it tastes just as good. Of course, if you get a piece of lean pork, that's better yet, because pork is usually too greasy. I don't love it. If you want to cut down on your budget, get a pig's head. Let the butcher cut it, not you, because it makes a mess. Wash the head, put some salt and boil it. After it boils, take off the meat, gristle and fat and mix it with the hamburger.

Then you mix everything together, hamburger, pork, salt, pepper, fennel, and you have real honest-to-goodness Italian sausage. You get a piece and roll it into shape with your hands. You don't have to have casing for shape. Then fry it and you'll have something really out of this world to taste. And it's simple. Absolutely nothing to making it. And people pay top price for that. That's the secret of the sausage: lots of black pepper, little bit pork lard and the rest hamburger.

How to make good stuffed artichokes. You get half a pound bread crumbs, five or six good-sized parsley leaves (I recommend German or Italian parsley, not the curly one), four or five beans of garlic, half a package Romano cheese. The 39-cent package kind. You put salt and pepper as it suits you and mix everything together. In this mixture, you put two or three eggs and about half a cup of water and mix all together. Then you get the artichokes and cut the tips about a quarter down from the end where the stickers are. Then you put your fingers on the end and open it up and stuff the artichokes with the mixture you made: bread crumbs, parsley, garlic, cheese, salt, pepper, eggs. If you like meat, you can put in half a pound of meat.

Cut off the stems of the artichokes, but don't throw them out because they're just as good as the artichokes themselves. Get a pot wide enough for as many artichokes as you have. Then you stand them up, stem side down, all the way around the inside of the pot and you put in no more than an inch or an inch and a half of water and you put some salt in the water. Put them on the stove with the lid on, and let it cook very slowly, steam cooked, for about an hour or an hour and a half. The way you can tell when it is cooked is to pull one of the leaves. If the leaf pulls up very easy, without struggling, the artichokes is cooked. You can take them out of the pot and serve them, and you'll have a meal that everybody likes and nobody will turn you down. And they ask you for the recipe.

Then if you want to make a good meal from the artichoke stems, get the inside from the bush before they start to make artichokes. We call it carduna (cardoon). Carduna is wild artichoke, and it's a little thick. I snap the leaves from the bottom of the trunk, I cut off all the leaves and leave the stem that is in the center. The stem looks like a celery. You wash and clean it, cut down to about 4- or 5-inch pieces, get a pot, fill it three quarters full of water, and boil the water. And when you boil it, you put lots of salt in the pot.

The carduna usually take from three quarters to one hour to cook. But don't put them in the water until the water is boiling. When they are cooked, put them under the faucet and rinse off all the salt. When they are well washed I usually put them back in the pot and let it boil again. The reason to put lots of salt is not because I like salt but because the salt cuts down all the bitterness in the stems. And that goes for any kind of vegetable that is bitter. Cook it in salt and wash it off until it tastes good.

After the stems are cooked, you get two or three cups of flour and one or one and a half packages of Romano cheese, about ten to fifteen good-sized parsley leaves, six to eight beans of garlic and chop it down good. In the flour, you put three eggs and mix it together. Then you get half a cake of yeast and melt it in half a cup of warm water. Then you put it in the flour and mix it all together and make like a paste. Of course, you put salt and pepper also.

When you have this all finished, you let it ferment, for about half an hour or three quarters. Then you take the stems and dip them in the flour mixture and deep fry them in olive oil. Let it brown on the bottom and then turn it over. If you do exactly like I say, you'll have a taste out of this world.

With this mixture you can also fry eggplant. First you cut your eggplant—or zucchini or pumpkin or other squash—in slices about half an inch thick. Put them on a dish and sprinkle each layer with salt, depending on how much you have. Put lots of salt. These things have lots of water and the salt draws it all out. I usually like good-sized zucchini, not the little stinky things you buy at the store. I get zucchini that is 3 to 4 inches diameter and about 10 or 12 inches long. I slice them and put salt on.

I let them sit about fifteen minutes to half an hour and the salt absorbs the water of the eggplant, zucchini or squash. Then I rinse them out good and squeeze them. Take all the water out. Then I dip them in the mixture for the artichoke stems and deep fry them. Boy-oh-boy, a meal like you never ate before.

Let's talk about how you make real, honest-to-goodness mushrooms. You get good-sized mushrooms. I usually pick them 3 to 4 inches wide. Wash them, but don't dry the water off, and don't drain them. I cut the stems and put them stem side up in a large pan. Sprinkle some pepper over, and then some salt, and put olive oil inside the cups of the mushrooms. I don't throw out the stems. I put them in the pan also. Put them in the broiler and let them cook about twenty minutes. When you take them out, let them cool off a little bit. Mmmmm, you have a good meal.

Now, suppose you want to make your own cheese, Romano or parmesan. The best cheese comes out of sheep milk, but where are you going to get sheep milk? But goat milk you can get most any place. Get a gallon or more of goat milk. See that the milk has never been in a refrigerator and see that it is raw milk. The best is right out of the goat. Then you get a rennet pill. That's a starter like yeast that comes from the stomach of baby goats. In Italy, Spain and Greece, they kill baby goats around Easter. They kill them before they are old enough to eat grass. The baby goat has a craw like a chicken which holds the milk. They take off the craw and, when it is dry, that's rennet. Melt the pill in a cup of warm milk and add it to the cold milk. For each gallon of milk, you put a good-sized teaspoon of salt or more. Make it way saltier than your taste.

Put it all in a good-size bowl and cover it up. I usually put it inside the stove, but I don't light the stove. The pilot light will keep it warm, because it has to be quiet and warm, not hot. Let it stay about one hour. Then you pull it out and put your finger in it and if your finger comes out dry, that's the time to use it. It looks like cottage cheese after one hour in the stove.

Then get a pint or pint and a half of boiling water and throw it in the cottage cheese. Put your hands very slowly on the edge of the bowl and move them toward the center very lightly. And keep adding boiling water. Pretty soon you make a ball out of there. When it is all one piece there will be water left over. Don't throw out the water because it can be used to make ricotta. Put the leftover water in a tin pan; it has to be tin to make ricotta.

To make ricotta, you have to make a little broom to stir up the water; otherwise it will burn the bottom of the pan and nothing will come out. You can make the broom out of any kind of palm. Put a stick in the center of a bunch of palm leaves and tie it in with string and cut it off 3 or 4 inches from the stick and make the tips even. That's your little broom for stirring up the water that came from the cheese.

Once you got the fire, stir it up very slowly on the bottom with the little broom and never stop stirring, until the ricotta comes up. When the water is just before the point of boiling, throw an extra glass of milk in the pot and stir it up. Never stop stirring. Before the water and the new milk start to boil, you'll have ricotta. And ricotta, if it is done the way I just said, you'll lick your fingers.

Put a pinch of salt in the water that came out of the cheese before you start to boil it, so you bring good taste. When the ricotta starts to come up, you stop stirring and lower the fire. That water never should boil, because if it does you won't get any ricotta. Then you get a little screen and scrape the ricotta out. If you have five gallons of water you'll get a good pound or two of ricotta. Put it in a ball and eat it whenever you want.

After you take the ricotta off, don't let the water cool off. Get the ball of cheese you been making before, put it in some cheesecloth, squeeze it into a nice tight ball and put it in the leftover water. Put it in while the water is still hot and let it stay there overnight. Then you take the cheese out and let it drain. Let it dry, but don't throw out the water. If you have any kind of animal, like a cat or dog, you can feed it to them. If you have a chicken, mix some food with it. Or if you want to have a real good breakfast, warm up some of that water and put in some bread or cereal. Boy, you never taste anything like it.

Now, when the cheese is dry for two or three days, melt some beeswax and before it hardens mix it with some olive oil and some salt until it is the consistency of butter. Spread this mixture with your hand all over the cheese as a seal. If it leaks, it will mold. It should age about three months. The longer it stays, the better it tastes.

Suppose you have been raising zucchini. Let the zucchini get about four or five pounds each. About 8 to 10 inches long and 4 or 5 inches across. Get it when it is tender, not old.

Cut the zucchini into ¼-inch thick slices. Put them in a pan and put a lot of salt on top. Then put another layer of zucchini and, on top of each layer, put salt until you use all the zucchini. Let the salt sink in for fifteen minutes.

Then peel two good-sized onions and take the skins off 2 pounds of tomatoes. Put the tomatoes with the onions and let them fry together. After they have been fried for fifteen or twenty minutes and the onions are brown, take the zucchini and wash the salt off. Then fry the zucchini in olive oil. Fry both sides of the zucchini until they are a little brown. Then put one layer of zucchini in a dish. Next, put some of the tomato-onion mixture. If you have some Romano cheese, put that too. And make one layer after another. Then it is ready to serve. One zucchini should serve four or five people. And everyone will enjoy it and it's simple to make and it costs less than a dollar and a half for five people.

RECIPES

Mixed Spices

Grind together 1 part each:
    celery seed
    parsley seed
    raw black peppers
    cayenne pepper
    adaghiro or bay leaves
    rose hips, seeds and petals
    sweet basil
    cloves
    cinnamon

Stuffed Artichokes

> ½ pound bread crumbs
> 2 or 3 eggs
> ½ package Romano cheese
> ½ cup water
> 4 or 5 beans of garlic
> 5 or 6 parsley leaves
> salt and pepper to taste

Mix together and stuff into artichokes. Steam cook with lid on for one to one and a half hours.

Artichoke Stems, Eggplant and Squash Dip

> 2 or 3 cups flour
> 1 or 1½ packages Romano cheese
> 10 to 15 parsley leaves
> 6 to 8 beans of garlic
> 3 eggs
> ½ cake yeast
> salt and pepper to taste

Mix and let rise for 30 to 45 minutes. Dip cooked stems or squash and deep fry in olive oil.

Italian Sausage

> 2 pounds hamburger
> large pinch fennel seed
> salt and pepper to taste (but more pepper than usual)
> ¼ pound pork meat or lard or cooked pig's head

Mix and roll into shape, and fry.

"Meatballs"

> 2 cups bread crumbs
> 1 cup ground fava beans
> 2 beans of garlic
> 3 or 4 eggs
> 3 or 4 ounces cheese
> 1 tablespoon parsley
> 4 ounces sardine or tuna

Cook with sauce for one hour.

Italian Sauce

> 30 pounds ripe tomatoes
> 3 pounds onions
> 4 ounces bay leaves
> 10 pounds ripe figs
> 4 ounces sweet basil
> 2 hot peppers
> salt to taste

Boil for at least three hours. Grind or blend everything but the bay leaves. Add 1 clove of garlic, browned in olive oil, and ¾ tablespoon mixed spices. Cook for another half hour.

Good Salad Dressing

> 1 cup vinegar (or lemon juice)
> 3 tablespoons olive oil
> 1 heaping tablespoon roquefort cheese
> 1 bean of garlic
> 1 tablespoon brown sugar or honey
> 2 full tablespoons tomato sauce or ketchup
> salt and pepper to taste

If you have a blender, blend it all together for one minute. If you put extra salt in, it will keep without refrigeration for a long time.

17

FIRE AND SLIDES

If you have your own farm, it is very important that you know how to protect yourself against natural disasters. First we talk about fire, the fire hazards, the plants and what to do when you have a fire and what to do to stop having fire.

The shrubs and trees which are fire hazards are those which have oil, like, for instance, the eucalyptus tree, pine tree, cypress tree, lemon tree, olive tree, juniper. All these particular trees that are fire hazards, I would chop down.

If you have a fireplace, you burn them. If you haven't got a fireplace, you make them into small pieces and you can sell them.

I would recommend that shrubs and trees with oil be kept at least 200 feet away from your house, so, in case of fire, you haven't got any problems and your house won't catch on fire.

Now, how can you know if a plant or tree has oil or not? You get a dry leaf that's been dropped from the plant and you put a match under it. You light the match and if the leaf sparks like a firecracker, that means the tree or shrub has oil and I wouldn't plant it near my house—or yours.

If you get the leaf, you put a match under it and if the leaf wrinkles, you don't have to worry about it. There's no oil in there. And that's the plant I would put near the house. There are a lot of plants you can put in. You don't have to put in oil plants near your house if they're fire hazards. Try to be safe. Don't say, "Oh, the fire's never going to come near here." You never can tell what is going to happen in the future.

Another thing I would do to prevent fires is to put sprinklers all over the house. Three, four, five sprinklers on the roof of the house. I would put them over the garage. And if there is any fire near, within two or three miles, open the sprinklers Wet the roof. Don't think because the fire is two miles away that your roof won't catch on fire. It will, because I have seen sparks in my experience travel five miles and burn and start a fire in a dry place. But if you put water on your roof, any spark that comes on your roof will be shut off.

Another thing I want to remind you, when a sprinkler is put on the roof, at least once a month you have to try it out to see if it works or not because them sprinklers they get corrosion, and the most important time when you want them, they don't work because the corrosion will stop them.

Now, another thing I do, always keep the house clear. Never have any shrubs or weeds within one hundred feet of the property where your house is, even if they don't belong to you. If they don't belong to you, call the state or county and they will clear it out for you and they charge it to the property owner, whoever it belongs to. It's got to be one hundred feet minimum. Another thing I want to remind you, if your house burns down because you have oil trees and you have insurance, the insurance never will pay you nothing because you're not covered.

I want to repeat this—if the shrubs and weeds don't belong to you, call the County Weed Abatement Department and they will come and plow them in and charge it to the property owner. If there is a fire hazard, they will do that.

Another thing I want to remind you, never keep a lot of trash and paper or anything flammable inside your garage. If you have paint, thinner, anything that can catch on fire, if you have room, put them away from your house. Out of the way.

So, if there is a chance of fire, even if you only have a little stream of water, you've got a chance to shut off the fire, but if you have a lot of stuff in the garage, you never can shut it off, specially if you have thinner or paint.

Don't look in my garage because my garage, the way it is now, it is a fire hazard. But nothing can catch on fire because I have much water on top of the roof. If the fire gets on my garage, I can shut it off easy.

Another thing I would do, if you have any important papers and the fire gets near where you are, and you are a fire hazard, even if the fire is ten miles away from your place, I would pick up all your important papers, jewelry, money if you have it, and I would make a hole in the ground. Put them inside a can or box and bury them in the ground not any less than two feet deep, because if it is a real strong fire it will burn under two feet.

You mark where you put them with a rock or a piece of steel or anything that couldn't be burnt. I have seen, sometimes, fire that won't leave any trace of anything that ever been there if the fire is strong enough. And when you come back to get your valuable papers and jewelry, whatever you have in there, you never could find it. But if you do have a rock or a piece of steel on the mark, you will find it without any trouble.

Now this is very important. If a fire came close to your

place, just like it did down here in Malibu, and it burned
all the shrubs on the hillside, you have to watch out for
slides when the next heavy rains come because the rain is more
dangerous than the fire is. You can stop the fire by sprinkling
the roof, but you can't stop the slide when it comes down.
Them houses go down in Malibu and nobody can save them.
But they could be stopped. There is no such thing as you can't.
What you do is, you make trenches from the edge of the
hillside running down.

You make two trenches. One on the top of the hillside and
let it curve down the hill so it doesn't run too fast and let the
trench drain out to level ground. Never leave the hillside
without any trenches. Then you make another trench about
ten feet away from the first trench. One trench would do, but
I want to be safe with two trenches. They don't have to be
such big trenches because the water will make its own trench.
You just have to guide it.

The reason for this trench is, when it rains and the water
comes down, it won't go straight down on the hillside and
wash your house out. Without any trench, little streams of
water go down from the hillside, and the little streams, they
make a big ditch, and if your house stands on the hillside,
it will slide. By making a trench in a circle and letting the
water go around the hillside, you save your house.

Also you make another trench near your house so you can
trap all the water that comes from your roof when it rains.
Let that water that comes from your roof go in a special
trench you make around your house. And you can connect
that trench with the other trenches that you made from the
hillside.

The water that comes down from the roof, that's the most
important trench you've got to make, because if you have a
house that is 2,500 square feet, you realize how much water
2,500 square feet collect. Twenty-five hundred square feet

Trenching for Proper Drainage

collect over three or four or six inches pipeline worth of water. And it always goes on the slope side, and soon the water makes a little trench himself and you're in trouble.

And the trenches you've been making before the rain, these trenches have to be absolutely clean. No leaves sitting in them. Before the rain, you clean up your trenches, because if you don't I'll tell you what is going to happen. Little branches get into the trench. The water brings down the leaves, and they stop on the little level spots that you have in the trenches. Another leaf stops and another leaf stops and pretty soon you get the whole trench clogged up and it will break on the side and take all your soil away.

But if you do like I say, you never will have a problem. You don't have to worry about it. I don't worry about fire. And the fires, believe me, they burn pretty close to my place.

I go to bed and sleep. How many people are there that live on a hillside where the fire is and they can sleep? Even if the fire is five miles away from them. They can't sleep because they're worried about the fire coming to burn their house. But if you do like I tell you to do, then you don't have to worry about it. You can go to bed and sleep.

By the way, one thing I don't do that the county and state do is after a fire they plant rye. That's the worst thing they ever do, because when they plant rye it's true that it stops slides, but next summer there will be high hay because the potash and the sunshine make the weeds grow high and then you have a worse fire hazard than you had the year before.

Now I will tell you how I know about fire.

In 1908, my family and I was in North Africa and the French government in Africa gave land on percentage. We used to get the land, clean up the woods and plant trees. We used to go fifty-fifty on the land with the government. And the government gave us the land for ten years.

One day there was a fire in the area where we was. It was

all woods. It happened in the nighttime and the gendarmes, the French policemen with horses, warned all the farmers in the woods that there was a fire about two miles away. Of course the wind was in the opposite way from where we was. It pushed the fire the other way. But still they warned all the people living in the woods, because we weren't the only ones who had this contract with the government to clean up the woods. There was a lot of people on ten years' contract. They warned us to get out of the house.

We had about six or seven acres cleaned up already, and my father took all the belongings that we had. We was eight in the family at the time, and we carried stuff to the center of the land that we had cleaned up. Then the wind came toward us and we was in the center of the cleared land. And the animals, all different kinds, came in there to be protected from the fire. Believe it or not, any animal, when he is in a fire, is so scared he won't look for food. They won't attack you. Until the fire was over we was just like a big family on the big piece of land that we cleaned out. The animals would fight each other, but they never touched us.

My father and the other men dug out holes in the cleaned land deep enough for us to stay so we didn't get burned. The heat was so hot that a cloth on the outside would burn just with the heat, not with the fire that came from the trees. The trees where we was were 100 to 125 feet high and all close together. It was exactly like a kiln. That's how hot it was.

When we was in the hole, the coolness from the earth protected us. Each family dug out their own hole. We was about five families on that particular space, on the cleaned land. That's about the most scariest life you ever had because no way can you get out. Especially when you got woods all the way around you.

My father put strict restrictions on the food and water. We had a quarter slice bread a day and one teaspoon of water three times a day. That's how we rationed the water and divided the food. This lasted over a month. Of course, the fire lasted three months, but it passed us. After it passed us, we had help from outside and we had food that was brought in.

Now when that fire passed our house, nothing was left. Absolutely nothing. Everything was burned down to the ground. Of course, the house was made out of wood, not like here where we have a foundation.

That's the experience that I have with fire, and I think very few people have the same experience, because you don't know if you're going to live or die or burn.

Now I'm going to tell a little bit about rain and floods. My father had a piece of property by a dry river near Palermo, in Sicily. It was about 200 feet away from the center of the river. He had lemon trees, orange trees, fig trees. We had a toolhouse made out of stone blocks, 1 foot by 1 foot by 18 inches long; we slept there when we were working in the fields. The trees were about 20 to 25 feet high and 18 to 20 feet spread. No one ever remembered that any water from the river ever reached that particular spot where my father had this property.

One time, it started to rain, and after it rained six days the water started to come out of the river. After eight days of raining, the water was higher than the trees and the toolhouse. We couldn't see the toolhouse or the trees. That particular time, it rained ten days. Not rain like we have around here in California. I actually saw the water bring down rocks as big as three-room houses. And it looked like it was a running lake.

Our house, our town, was way on the top of a hill. In Italy you never see towns on level ground like we have around here. Most of them towns are up on the hills. Our trees weren't the only ones that was covered by the water. All the people that had farms there had them covered with water. And the water kept draining from the mountains for eighteen days after it stopped raining. Then it started to slow down and the water released the land and went back to the center of the river. We couldn't get to our property for forty-five days.

It took all the trees that we had. Pulled them right out. It took the toolhouse made out of big solid blocks. Took it right out into the ocean. There was a highway bridge and it pulled it right out. There was a railroad bridge and it pulled it right out. Now, this is an experience that you couldn't forget about. I only was twelve or thirteen years old.

From then on, I watch and look at all the details before I go live any place. If it is not safe, I never stay there. Now that I am old enough to know what causes troubles like fire, slides and floods and I am old enough to buy property, I never buy property that is in danger from water, slides, flood or fire. I always protect myself. I never leave shrubs near my house that are fire hazards, and I always make trenches around my house so the water drains out. Of course, we can't say there is no danger, because sometimes, no matter how you protect yourself, if you got to go with the fire, you will go, and if you got to go with the water, you will go also. But I do try to protect myself to don't be burned by the fire if I can help it, or drowned with the water. Before you can farm you have to make sure your life and home and land are safe.

And this is Frank Bucaro talking, and everybody know me by Chico.

CHARTS

PLANTING TABLE

These figures are to be used as guidelines rather than rigid rules because all figures are subject to many variables. It is more useful to pay attention to the plants than to the numbers.

Plant	Distance Between Rows	Distance Between Plants in Row	Depth to Plant	Days to Harvest	Moon Phase or Quarter*	Sign†
Asparagus	3′	18″	Seed, ½″ Cutting, 4″	From seed, 3 yr. cutting, 1 yr.	1	C S P
Beans, fava	3′	6–8″	2″	90	2	C S P L T
Beans, lima	3′	3′	Bush, ½″ Pole, 1″	Bush, 70–90 Pole, 90	Bush 2 1, 2	C S P L T S
Beets	3′	8–10″	½″	90	3	C S P L Cap
Broccoli	3′	12″	Seed, ½″ Plant, to 1st leaf	90–120	1	C S P L
Brussels Sprouts	3′	12″	½″	90	1	C S P L

Cabbage	3'	10"	½"	90–120	1	C S P L T
Cantaloupe	3'	3'	1"	over 100	1,2	C S P L
Carrots	3'	Sprinkle seeds and thin later	½" (¾" at most)	80	3	C S P L
Cauliflower	3'	12"	Seed, ½" Plant, to 1st leaf	85–100	1	C S P L
Celery	3'	6–8"	2"	90	2	C S P L
Corn	3'	6"	1"	90	1	C S P
Cucumbers	3–5'	4'	½"	100–120	1	C S P
Eggplant	3'	8"	½"	80	2	C S P L
Endive	3'	8"	½"	70–90	1	C S P L V Sag
Kale	3'	12"	½"	90	1	C S P L
Kohlrabi	3'	8–10"	½"	90	1	C S P L
Lettuce	3'	8–10"	½"	Leaf lettuce, 60–70 Iceberg, 90–100	1	C S P L T
Onions	3'	6–8"	½"	60–90	2	S Sag

141

* Moon Phase or Quarter
1 & 2 – New moon to full moon
3 & 4 – Full moon to new moon

† Key to Sign Abbreviations
C = Cancer   T = Taurus
S = Scorpio   Cap = Capricorn
P = Pisces   Sag = Sagittarius
L = Libra   V = Virgo

PLANTING TABLE (*Continued*)

Plant	Distance Between Rows	Distance Between Plants in Row	Depth to Plant	Days to Harvest	Moon Phase or Quarter*	Sign†
Oyster plants (Salsify)	3′	6–8″	½″	90	1, 2	C S P
Parsley	3′	4–6″	½″	60–90	1	C S P L
Parsnips	3′	8–10″	½″	60–90	3	C S P L
Peanuts	1½–2′	18″	2″	120–150	3	C S P L
Peas, Sweet	3′	Bush, 18″ Pole, 3–5′ (If plant is tied to pole, 18″)	½″	60	2	C S P L
Peppers	3′	18″	½″	90–120	2	S Sag
Potatoes	3′	18–24″	1½–2″	90–120	3	C S T L Cap Sag
Radishes	3′	2–3″	½″	45–60	3	L T P Cap Sag

				Days	Moon Phase*	Sign†
Rutabagas	3'	10"	½"	90	3	C S P T
Spinach	3'	Sprinkle seeds and thin later	½"	45–90	1	C S P
Squash, summer	3–5'	3–5'	1"	90–120	2	C S P L
Squash, winter	4–5'	3–5'	1"	120	2	C S P L
Strawberries	3'	12"	Cover roots	From seed, 1–2 yrs. Plant, 90	3	C S P
Sweet potatoes	3'	3–5'	2–3"	180		
Swiss chard	3'	12"	1"	60–90	1, 2	C S P L
Tomatoes	3'	3–5'	Seed, ½" In row, to 1st leaf	90–120	2	C S P
Turnips	3'	8–10"	½"	60–90	3	C S P T Cap L
Watercress	3'	Sprinkle seeds in water	Sprinkle seeds in water	90	1	C S P
Watermelons	3–5'	3–5'	1"	100	1, 2	C S P L

143

* Moon Phase or Quarter
1 & 2 – New moon to full moon
3 & 4 – Full moon to new moon

† Key to Sign Abbreviations
C = Cancer   T = Taurus
S = Scorpio   Cap = Capricorn
P = Pisces   Sag = Sagittarius
L = Libra   V = Virgo

FROST

Plants that stand sharp frost: plant as soon as soil can be worked.

Asparagus	Carrots	Kohlrabi	Rhubarb
Beets	Endive	Parsnips	Rutabagas
Broccoli	Kale	Radishes	Turnips
Cabbage			

Plants that stand light frost: plant when danger of soil freezing is past.

Brussels sprouts	Peas
Cauliflower	Radishes
Lettuce	Strawberries

Plants that cannot stand frost: plant when frost is no longer expected.

Beans	Eggplants	Potatoes	Tomatoes
Cantaloupes	Melons	Spinach	Watercress
Corn	Oyster plants	Squash	
Cucumbers	Peppers	Sweet potatoes	

GARDENING BY THE MOON

For thousands of years human beings have known that the Moon has a great effect on the way plants grow. To test these techniques, plant half of your garden by the Moon and half at random. Treat both halves with equal love. (For additional information read *The Moon Sign Book*, Llewellyn Publications, Box 3383—MSB, Saint Paul, Minnesota 55165.)

BIENNIALS—Crops that are planted one season, allowed to grow through winter and harvested the next season. An example is winter wheat.

PERENNIALS, BULB AND ROOT PLANTS—Plants that grow from the same root year after year.

ANNUALS—Plants that complete their entire life cycle in one growing season and have to be seeded anew each season. There are basically two kinds of annuals: LEAFY ANNUALS that produce their seed outside the fruit, and VINY ANNUALS that produce their seed inside the fruit.

Some LEAFY ANNUALS: asparagus, broccoli, brussels sprouts, cabbage, cauliflower, celery, cress, endive, kohlrabi, lettuce, parsley, spinach.

Some VINY ANNUALS: beans, eggplants, melons, peas, peppers, pumpkins, squash, tomatoes.

PLANTING BY THE MOON'S PHASES
INCREASING LIGHT (*from New Moon to Full Moon*)

1st QUARTER—plant LEAFY ANNUALS and cucumbers.

2nd QUARTER—plant VINY ANNUALS except cucumbers.

EITHER QUARTER—plant cereals, grains, watermelons, garlic and hay.

(It is safe to plant LEAFIES during the 2nd quarter and VINIES during the 1st quarter).

DECREASING LIGHT (*from Full Moon to New Moon*)

3rd QUARTER—plant biennials, perennials and bulb and root plants such as trees, shrubs, berries, beets, carrots, onions, parsnips, peanuts, potatoes, radishes, rhubarb, rutabagas, strawberries, turnips, grapes, etc.

4th QUARTER—best for cultivation, pulling weeds, discouraging pests, turning sod, especially when the Moon is in a barren sign.

PLANTING BY THE MOON'S SIGNS

Moon In:

ARIES: Barren and dry, fiery and masculine—destroy noxious growths, weeds, pests; also cultivate.

TAURUS: Productive and moist, earthy and feminine—plant for hardiness; root crops and leafy vegetables.

GEMINI: Barren and dry, airy and masculine—destroy noxious growths, weeds, pests; also cultivate.

CANCER: Very fruitful and moist, watery and feminine—best sign for planting and irrigation.

LEO: Barren and dry, fiery and masculine—most barren sign; destroy or cultivate.

VIRGO: Barren and moist, earthy and feminine—cultivate and destroy.

LIBRA: Semifruitful and moist, airy and masculine—plant for good pulp growth and roots; good for flowers and vines, good for seeding hay and corn fodder.

SCORPIO: Very fruitful and moist, watery and feminine, nearly as productive as CANCER—plant for vine growth and sturdiness.

SAGITTARIUS: Barren and dry, but good for planting onions and seeding hay, fiery and masculine—good for cultivation.

CAPRICORN: Productive and drier than TAURUS, earthy and feminine—plant potatoes, tubers, etc.

AQUARIUS: Barren and dry, airy and masculine—cultivate and destroy.

PISCES: Very fruitful and moist, watery and feminine—plant especially for root growth.

Most productive signs to plant: CANCER, SCORPIO, PISCES.
Next best, especially for root crops: TAURUS, CAPRICORN.
Next best: LIBRA, SAGITTARIUS, AQUARIUS.

WHEN TO DO WHAT Besides Planting

CULTIVATION AND TURNING SOD: Moon in barren sign, decreasing light—4th quarter best.

FERTILIZING (organic): Moon in fruitful sign, 3rd or 4th quarter.

FLOWERS: Plant during increasing light—LIBRA for beauty, CANCER, SCORPIO or PISCES for abundance, SCORPIO for sturdiness, TAURUS for hardiness.

HARVESTING:

ROOT CROPS FOR FOOD—3rd or 4th quarters and dry sign.

ROOT CROPS FOR SEED—at Full Moon

GRAIN TO BE STORED OR FOR SEED—after Full Moon, avoid watery signs.

FRUIT—3rd or 4th quarters and dry sign

IRRIGATION: When the Moon is in a watery sign.

MUSHROOMS: Best gathered at Full Moon.

PRUNING: During decrease—3rd quarter and SCORPIO are best to retard branch growth and make better fruit.

SPRAYING, WEEDING and OTHER DESTRUCTION: Moon in barren sign—4th quarter.

TRANSPLANTING: Same as planting.

INDEX